The
EARN
Method

Performing with Purpose

Sherri Sutton and William Casale

Positive Impact Force
4002 West State Street, Suite 200
Tampa, FL 33609
(727) 480-4145

This book is a work of non-fiction. Unless otherwise noted, the author and the publisher make no explicit guarantees as to the accuracy of the information contained in this book and in some cases, names of people and places have been altered to protect their privacy.

ISBN: 978-1-6847-0054-7 (sc)
ISBN: 978-1-6847-0019-6 (e)

Library of Congress Control Number: 2019904012

Lulu Publishing Services rev. date: 06/20/2019

Contents

Introduction

Do you enjoy your job? Do you wake up every morning and say, "I can't wait to go to work?" Do you love your boss, or are you just biding time to get away from him/her? Are you proud to say you work where you work? If the answers to these questions are yes, then you will love learning more about how you can perform with purpose in your organization. If the answers are no, then this book will help guide you to find your purpose, whether it is in your current organization or in your future organization.

It seems like most of the books out there today on how to succeed in business are geared toward leaders and business owners. Today's workforce is quickly changing with baby boomers transitioning out, millennials coming on board, and Gen Xers somewhere in the middle. There are not enough Gen Xers out there to fill the leadership roles, which is creating a critical need for employees who can link their performance to the overall vision of the organization without a manager watching them.

As business professionals who have managed large and small organizations, startups, speedboats, and battleships, we understand the heart and soul of any business is how well the people in it perform.

Sherri has spent most of her career working with leaders and one thing she knows well is that it is hard to shift someone who's already there. It seems the further up the ladder the leader moves, the less they want to engage in learning and changing. No matter where you are in your career or your life, learning is always a crucial component, and if you find yourself thinking that you already know everything, we invite you to sound your own alarm. Thinking you know everything is a clear sign you are stuck, and most likely need to seek objective feedback. Are you familiar with the parable, "*The Emperor's New Clothes?*" In the story, a tailor sells the emperor a nonexistent suit. He proudly parades around naked asking everyone if they like his new clothes. Afraid to upset him, everyone tells him he looks great. We have seen that scenario played out many times in the course of our careers. In our current *industrial age* leadership hierarchy, executive leaders receive very little feedback and generally, their staff tells them what they feel they want to hear. People put on their "talking to my boss" façade and dance around anything that can be perceived as negative, often leaving leaders to make decisions with little or incorrect information to make those decisions. The information is available, but the employees do not feel comfortable sharing it. Sherri believes if you change your leadership structure and invite your employees to co-create the most effective structure possible for your organization, you get better communication, more feedback, and better results. To do this, you need employees who can think and act like business owners, and the only way they can do this is through learning and development. These are not intuitive skills and they are not taught in the K-12 education system. However, they can be easily taught to anyone, which is the concept for this book. Great employees don't need to be managed, they need to be led, and great leaders don't want to manage. So, if we can reach and teach this audience, a new corporate hierarchy can emerge.

Our advice may not help everyone. Let's face it, sometimes employees are in the wrong positions, sometimes they lack clear direction, sometimes their skills don't align, sometimes their values don't align, sometimes they just need to take a time out to focus on what they want, and sometimes they just can't listen to any feedback. But this content isn't for those employees.

Early in his career, Bill gained experience with large corporate environments in the financial services sector. He also has been an entrepreneur, starting a consulting business that worked with large law practices and other professional services firms. He started an offshore outsourcing platform in Central America that employed over 1,000 employees, served on for-profit and non-profit advisory boards, and even owned and operated a cigar factory! The breath of his experience has taught him some fundamental truths that you will read about in this book. He believes in having plans and guidelines that outline business strategy, but also leaving room for employees to use their intuition, innovation, and expertise to achieve results. He also believes that no matter what part of the planet you are standing on, people who work with and for you need to know what is expected, how they are doing, and must be reinforced for the positive results that meet those expectations.

We have been manager and owner, served shareholders, board members, and worked as employees. We have seen great management and poor management. During our careers, we have had great successes and our share of failures. This experience helped us create some great strategies for success, some of which are included in this book. The EARN Method is just one strategy you will be exposed to in this book to help you analyze and manage your tasks. EARN stands for *end, automate, reassign,* and *nurture.* We have used EARN in many industries with employees and leaders, and it always yields results. Observing what happens if you *end* a task is very telling; knowing if you can *automate* it can save you time, money, and even save you from performing tasks you don't enjoy doing. This allows you to focus your attention on things that only humans can do to move your business forward. Evaluating if you can *reassign* a task can make sure the most qualified person is performing the task, and knowing where to *nurture* or spend your time and energy is vital to being successful. We'll talk more about how and when to use EARN and give you some examples of how we've used it throughout this book.

We will also discuss ways to organize your work life and perform your tasks to get results that should advance your career, and what to do when you reach hurdles, bumps, and walls that may get in the way of your success.

Bill says you need great vision or great pain to change, and we've discovered working with someone in great pain is exhausting, and can be, well ... a real pain! Working with people with vision is inspiring, energizing, and enlightening. Your vision should be to avoid the pain and embrace the possibilities.

Leaders are only as good as the people they lead, so we decided to design a book to help employees perform with purpose, regardless of the leader they are assigned to in their organization. Our method can also work for leaders who want to be sure their followers are on the same path. In most cases, anyone who is getting a check for doing something, whether they are the owner or not, can benefit from our methodology. Most people in charge think these things don't apply to them because they "made it" to a leadership position. Getting there is only part of the journey; staying there and enjoying it is quite another matter.

This material is intended for anyone who is fighting the good fight and earning their pay in search of the American dream. You may be a leader, or not ever want to be a leader; either way, we're pretty sure you don't want to hear anyone say you get a check and that's your reward. You EARN your check and you both want and deserve to work in an environment where you feel valued and provide value. Let's face it, without you, your company couldn't be profitable. Companies are great because of the performance of their people. We want to help you understand how important you are in the equation and how to help business owners live up to saying, "Our people are our greatest asset."

We sometimes refer to sports analogies throughout our stories and we like to think an organization should train like a football team. The coaches prepare the plays (in an organization this would be the goals) and then they spend hours and hours having the team practice, and making sure everyone on the team knows what to do and when. I wonder what would happen if all leaders considered themselves coaches?

Now don't get us wrong, the following pages are not guaranteed to make you a million dollars, restore your hair, or help you lose that stubborn belly fat. This book is only intended to empower you with a better understanding of business, allow you to develop productive ideas to share with your manager or owner, and make your job more enjoyable. This isn't a test run; this is your life, and we want you to live it completely. Focusing on hump day and saying TGIF is not living; it's wishing away five out of seven days a week. Bill's a big fan of saying, "how you do anything is how you do everything." We want to make sure you are focusing on how you're living because these could be the best years of your life, and you spend the best part of most days at work.

This book is designed to be an interactive experience for you, and how you choose to navigate it is up to you. In each chapter, we will outline Points of Impact that will provide an overview of the topics covered, along with activities and accompanying worksheets you'll be asked to download to assist in your learning. You can work through the book as you go, give it a quick read, and come back to it, or just do the parts you feel are relevant to you. Our recommendation is to work through it as you go so you can build on your knowledge. As you work through the material, you will find there is more than one way to achieve being an employee with purpose and having a positive impact.

There are thousands of books by scholars, experts, and charlatans all purporting to have the secret to business success. We don't have that. We do have years of experience doing things right and making mistakes (oh boy, have we made some doozies), working with and for some amazing people, and working with and for some real tools. At the end of the day, we mostly did more things right than wrong, and found some things that work well and are sustainable. There is no perfect approach or system. Most of the stuff you find in these types of books are just different flavors of the same ice cream. We hope you find our flavor cool and refreshing, take advantage of the flexibility to create your own flavor, and for goodness sake, don't drop your cone!

Since we put this book together and combined our stories, experience, and expertise, we will simply tell the story in the first person from here on; combining our voices into one, and each taking credit for each other's work (mostly because we forgot which parts we individually contributed). As you'll see, we provide our email address and website so you can contact us with questions and comments. We look forward to connecting with you and hearing your story as you work through this book, finding your favorite flavor, and identifying what works for you.

Acknowledgements

We would like to thank the many people we've worked with over the years. We've had the opportunity to cross paths with some amazing leaders, wise mentors and outstanding colleagues.

We'd also like to recognize the many people who read and gave us feedback as we worked through the material. Your input is invaluable.

Thank you to our editor, Gina Carrillo, for her many suggestions, need for clarification and working with our timeline.

CHAPTER 1
What You Do

In this chapter, the Positive Impact Points we will review include:

- Why you do what you do
  - The importance and relevance of your work
- The policies and procedures in your department
  - The written documentation you use to know what steps to follow when doing your job
- Training documentation and measurements
  - The documentation you use to know how to do your job and how your performance will be measured
- Analyzing job tasks and making sure they matter
  - Understanding how your job functions fit into the larger system in your organization
- The EARN Method: End, Automate, Reassign, Nurture

The worksheets you'll need include:

- Job Description Worksheet
- Critical Function Worksheet
- Training and Measurement Worksheet
- EARN Worksheet
- The Handy Dandy (and Incomplete) List of Questions

You can find worksheets here: www.earnmethodbook.com.

Now, let's get started with where your day begins.

When you go into work each morning, are you consciously aware of the choices you make and the language you use? What exactly is your job? Do you use your strengths doing it? How did you learn it? Did someone explain it to you? Did you have a manual or written policies and procedures? Did you receive training? Was it passed on to you like ancient wisdom by sitting next to a buddy? Or were you assigned to "Shirley", the wizened sage of the organization, who takes on all the new recruits, talks faster than you even knew possible, and skips over half the steps in her explanations because she has done her job for so long she forgets to mention things?

Regardless of how you learned your job, you show up every day and do what you do. I'm a bit of an optimist, but I believe most people wake up most days with the intent to be the best person they can be and come into work wanting to do a great job. Arguably, some days you perform better than others, and even if your training wasn't good, eventually you figure out how to do the work, which often times is not even the same way you were originally taught. In this chapter, I want you to take a hard look at all the things you do, analyzing their relevance, whether they are necessary, important, vital, or wasteful. It's essential to know if the work you do has relevance today, or if you were taught to do some things because that's the way it's always been done. I encourage you to ask who is using the information; to make the conscious choice of determining if what you do matters to your company *today*. I'll talk more about what questions to ask and how to ask the right questions in the next chapter.

I also want you to be aware of what you do best. What does the SportsCenter highlight reel of your day look like? What duties do you just shrug your shoulders and perform, scratching your head, wondering why you even bother? For example, reports you run, fields you populate in a system, forms you file, mail you receive, phone calls you make, and so on. The best way for you to help your company is for you to understand why you do what you do, and how it fits into the overall products or services your company offers. I have devised some simple ways for you to analyze your activities and identify ways to make your day more productive and fulfilling.

Let's first look at where you work. Do you work in a department, division, team, or some other sort of unit that somehow contributes to the overall success of the company? If you describe what your group does in a couple of sentences, what does it look like? If you had to explain it to a new person coming to work with you, what would you say? For example, if you were on the Learning and Development team, you might write something like this:

> *"We offer timely, accurate, measurable, and just-in-time learning solutions that align with the organization's goals. This position is responsible for new-hire orientation, e-learning, instructor-led training (ILT), and supporting management as requested. A member of the Learning and Development team attends all leadership, steering, and business development meetings, and has the opportunity to be a voice for all learners. We contribute to the overall success of the organization by ensuring our employees have the information they need when they need it."*

If your organization is well versed in job descriptions, it may be more specific, for example, stating what timely means or defining accuracy.

Most organizations have multiple types of units: **support** units, like HR, Learning & Development, Facilities, IT, and Accounting that are the backbone of the business and are necessary for day-to-day operations; **operational** or **production** units that either perform a service or produce a product; and **customer-centric** units, like Sales, Marketing, and call or order centers. In smaller companies, these roles are often combined, or one person is responsible for several of these functions. You should be able to identify where you fit in, and it is okay if you choose more than one role.

Now, think about your role, where you are in the organization, and what you do to support the organization every day. Try to be as descriptive as you can by summing up what you are doing in a single paragraph that speaks to the importance of you, your team, and its contribution to the whole. Be bold and brag. This is not a time to be bashful. Exactly how do you make a positive difference? Let's say you're a cashier in a grocery store. How can a cashier make a positive difference in your day? I just went grocery shopping this week and when I was checking out, the cashier was friendly, smiled, asked me questions, and shared her energy. She seemed to be bursting with energy and connected with each customer. As I walked out of the store, I noticed I had a little more lift in my step just from going through her line. So, if she were answering this question, she might say, "My job is to make everyone's day a little better when they shop at our store. I connect with people and I share stories so they feel seen. I also ring up their purchases and pass them to someone to bag while I collect their money." Often, we have a job (tasks) but we *do* so much more! It's doubtful her job description really states all that she does for the customers who go through her line.

Get ready for your first activity! If you don't already have it open, pull up the **Job Description Worksheet** you downloaded at the beginning of this chapter, and type how you'd describe what you do and how you make people feel. If you haven't downloaded the worksheet yet, you can find it here: www.earnmethodbook.com.

How did that go? From the looks of your worksheet, I'm going to guess you're pretty important to your organization. I can say that because I know if you weren't the type of person who would go the extra mile, you wouldn't be reading this book.

Now that you've reflected on your value, let's take a look at the nuts and bolts of what you do every day. In public transportation, it is very important for the trains to run on time. If people can't rely on the transportation to get them where they are going on time, they won't use it. Thinking about this analogy, what trains need to run on time in your business? What is your role in making that happen? What are the core functions, that if not completed accurately and timely, will have a detrimental impact on your company's business? Yes, I know you may not be a leader and you are not privy to all of your organization's information. Think about what you do know and what information you do have, and then answer the questions to the best of your ability. You'll need this information a little later when you'll be asked to share this information with your leader and talk about how you feel you are contributing to the business. If there are gaps in your knowledge, your leader can help provide that information. As a leader, I loved having these conversations with my staff because only exemplary employees want to talk about their contribution to the business.

Throughout this book, you'll be prompted to ask a lot of questions of your boss and your leaders. I want to emphasize that I am not suggesting you challenge your boss and refuse to do what they ask you to do. Timing is everything, so look for the appropriate time to ask your question or make a suggestion. Some questions are great for a group setting, others are better for one-on-one time. If you have a hunch that the answer may upset or embarrass the person you are asking, always do this in a one-on-one setting. Nobody likes a "know-it-all", so frame your questions from a position of curiosity rather than inquisition or superiority. Unfortunately, know-it-alls don't generally know it all, and they are unaware that they are acting like a know-it-all, so to quote Ice Cube, "check yourself before you wreck yourself." One way to do this is to consider the response you are getting from the person you are talking to. If they appear annoyed or upset, you need to try another approach. Remember, the goal is to build your curiosity around what you are doing so you can ask great questions. Later, I will share stories from my experience on how these questions saved or could have saved a lot of time, money, and morale.

To prepare for your meeting, use the Critical Function Worksheet you downloaded at the beginning of this chapter to document the reoccurring critical functions that are vital to the success of your business, along with some other key information. Don't worry about getting into extreme detail in every step you perform, but rather, think high-level overview of the function.

Using the cashier scenario as an example, the worksheet would look something like this:

\multicolumn{6}{c}{Critical Function Worksheet – Checking out a Customer}					
Priority	Critical Function	Procedure in Place (Y/N)	Measurement in Place (Y/N)	Performance Meets Expectations (Y/N)	Opportunities for Improvement (Y/N)
	Smile and be friendly	N	N	Y	Y
	Get to know people – connect with the regular shoppers	N	N	Y	Y
	Scan grocery items	Y	Y	Y	N
	Manually key in items that won't scan	Y	Y	Y	N
	Manage payments	Y	Y	Y	N
	Bag groceries if no one is available to assist	Y	Y	Y	Y
	Sweep store during slower hours	Y	Y	Y	Y

Notice the focus is on what the cashier's most important role is, not necessarily the job description itself.

Now, it's your turn. If you haven't already, open the **Critical Function Worksheet** and complete the following steps:

STEP 1: Start by making a list of all the tasks you do daily, weekly, and monthly that make up your job. I suggest you first write down as many critical functions as you can think of that you perform in your job. Think about how you perform your role, who you interact with, and all the steps you do to get it done. Then, type them in the form and as you do, continuing to add additional rows as needed to your worksheet. Are you surprised by all that you do? Do you find it enlightening? Are you seeing how important you are to your customers, boss, and company? Are there any critical functions you wrote down, but when you look at it in writing, you wonder why you do it? For example, it could be something that may have been replaced by automation, is duplicate work, or may be a of an executive who left the organization a long time ago. An example might be that you are printing a form from a computer system and mailing it when the form is automatically emailed to the client as a scanned form. I have seen many organizations spend thousands of dollars in postage doing this. Take a moment and see if you see anything on your list that may not be necessary.

STEP 2: Next, determine which of your critical functions are the top three most important and in the **Priority** column, type **1**, **2**, or **3** next to each of your picks.

If you feel your boss would rank your tasks differently, make a note and when you meet with your boss, discuss why you feel your top picks are important. The only way to perform with purpose is to have a voice and be able to communicate your thoughts and feelings in a productive way. Sometimes, when you talk with your boss and get more information, you may change your mind on how you rank tasks, which is fine. And sometimes, when your boss understands why you ranked them this way, they will change their mind.

STEP 3: In the **Procedure in Place** column, enter **Y** (yes) or **N** (no) to indicate whether there is a procedure in place for each of your critical functions. A procedure is a written document that lists the step-by-step activities you need to perform to complete that critical function. If you're not sure, leave it blank.

STEP 4: In the **Measurement in Place** column, enter **Y** (yes) or **N** (no) to indicate if there are metrics in place to measure your performance for each of your critical functions.

STEP 5: In the **Performance Meets Expectations** column, enter **Y** (yes) or **N** (no) to indicate if you believe your job performance for each of your critical functions meets your manager's expectations. If you are not sure how your performance stacks up, this is a great time to discuss this with your manager or supervisor. If they are not sure, then you have a great opportunity to define what "meeting expectations" looks like. This will also help you define step 4.

STEP 6: Lastly, in the **Opportunities for Improvement** column, enter **Y** (yes) or **N** (no) to indicate if you believe you have any opportunities for improvement.

Excellent work! I love your energy and your desire to take control of your job and your company. Share this list with your coworkers, managers, and others you interact with, and complete any blank boxes together. This is a great learning opportunity for you!

Next, let's focus on how you do what you do. You may think it's odd to be concerned about how you do your job, since that seems more like your company's responsibility. But, if you want to perform with purpose and control your own destiny, you must make sure you receive the proper training to do things correctly. If you learned the job yourself, but don't have any documented training for your position, talk to your manager about creating it. It could be a training manual, videos, or documents stored on a shared drive. No matter the format, just make sure your job is documented. Why? Because if you are not able to go to work tomorrow, someone else can do your job. I know you plan to be at work every day, but accidents happen, opportunities occur, and sometimes people don't make it work. So, be sure you have written documentation for your job that is accessible and updated.

Another benefit of documenting training for your job is that it allows you to easily train someone else to do your job, should you need a backup so you can take vacation or you take a promotion in another department. I've seen some exemplary employees overlooked for promotions because their boss didn't want to go through the headache of replacing them and having to teach someone else to do their job. In the process of documenting your position and making sure you have written training, you will often uncover tasks you do not need to do anymore, or easy measurements you can put in place. For example, the cashier in the grocery store might document asking each customer if they found everything they were looking for. She would then ask the manager what the procedure is if the customer says no, and if the manager wants to measure how many customers couldn't find what they were looking for. Why would that be important? What if 20-30% of the customers are looking for the same things? Or, what if 40% of customers can't find what they are looking for? This could be very valuable information for the cashier and her manager. I hope you are starting to see just how valuable you can be to your company!

To start this process, think about what training is currently available for your job function and how it is measured. If you have a training department that takes care of this for you, be sure to smile and thank them because you'll have much less work to do in this section. However, there are still tasks and functions that you perform that are most likely not covered in initial training. So, take a moment to think about the things that are not covered in training and record them. Going back to the grocery store example, if all new-hires are trained how to scan food items and what to do if there isn't a code to scan, that should cover 95% of the items. However, if there are also new items that come in that have never been sold before, like furniture, gloves, cleaners, and wooden reindeers, that should be included in future training.

Essentially, once you learn how to do something or run across a unique situation, document it, for example, customer service issues that you were the first to encounter. Basically, if you do it, document it. Having your own secret sauce is a great way to have special recipes to share with family and friends, but it is not helpful in your job. You don't want to keep information to yourself and be the only one who can handle certain situations. I know it seems like it could make you valuable and important to your company, but what it really does is hinder your ability to be as successful as you can be for two reasons: 1) You become the "go- to" person to handle anything associated with that knowledge, which can keep you from learning new skills. 2) Other employees withhold information from you. Long term, it is better to document your job position, overshare, and be collaborative. Your objective is to be able to train someone else to do your job.

Training documentation doesn't have to be fancy; it needs to be efficient. So, think of an easy way to both document training and measure what you are doing. I'm a firm believer that you can measure the performance for any job. I worked with a group of legal assistants one time who were adamant there was no way to measure their work. They stated they did different tasks every day and their day revolved around what the attorney needed. I asked them how they knew they were doing a good job and they said that if the attorney was happy, they were doing a good job. After we analyzed the work they did and what it took for them to be efficient, they were able to identify several meaningful measurements they could use in their job. Some examples are:

- Drafting a letter to opposing counsel for XXX in 10 minutes
- Reviewing the attorney's calendar every morning by 8:00 A.M. and alerting the attorney by 8:10 A.M. of any changes, meetings, or items due that day
- Schedule all hearings for attorney in XXX county by 12:00 P.M. each day

They didn't know how many letters they would draft daily, but they did know how long it should take and were able to come up with individual tasks to measure.

As you think about documenting training for your job, how do the measurements relate to that? Wow, you were very quick to answer that, and you are right. You want to make sure the training teaches the learner how to do the job function to achieve the measurement. You can teach someone how to draft a letter to the opposing counsel, but you need to make sure you teach them how to do it within 10 minutes, if that is how they will be measured.

Now, let's take a look at the questions you want to ask yourself when reviewing or creating the training for your position. If you haven't already downloaded the **Training and Measurement Worksheet**, do that now and complete the following steps.

STEP 1: On page 1, review each of the questions, check off those that apply, and determine if you need to talk to your manager and/or create the needed training documentation.

STEP 2: On page 2, use the space provided to answer each of the questions.

STEP 3: Review the worksheet and determine if you have any other questions or need any additional information. If you do, write the information down to discuss with your manager.

Training and Measurement Worksheet

- Do you have a written procedure or instruction on how and when to perform your job function? If yes, check the box.
  If no, do one of the following:
  - o Talk to your manager about creating one
  - o Create a procedure or instruction on how and when to perform your job function
- Is there a manual, checklist, video, or some other documentation that demonstrates how to perform the work? If yes, check the box.
  If no, do one of the following:
  - o Talk to your manager about creating one
  - o Create a procedure or instruction on how and when to perform your job function

- Does your training explain the overall purpose of the job function and how to perform each task, why you do what you do, and how it effects other functions and departments? If yes, check the box.
  If no, do one of the following:
  - o Talk to your manager about creating one
  - o Create a procedure or instruction on how and when to perform your job function
- ☐ How are you measuring what you do? If you are not currently measuring your job, what are your ideas on how your job can be measured?
- ☐ Are there benchmarks, expectations, or standards for your job position? Are they documented or unspoken?
- ☐ When you get your performance review (assuming you get a performance review), how is your performance rated?
- If you don't get a performance review, how do you rate yourself?
- How do you know if what you are doing is timely, properly done, and so on? What is the basis for comparison?

Does this seem like a lot of work to you? Are you wondering why you would do all of this work when you have a manager? It's a fair question. My standard answer is that you don't need a manager, you need a leader. The more you understand about your job, how to do it, how it is measured, and why you do what you do, the better you can determine the best way to do the job. Then, if you run into difficulties or need help, your leader can help you maneuver any of those obstacles. The only way you can have strong leaders to help you is if you can manage the daily function of your job yourself, and you are the best person to manage your work because you understand it the best.

Think about it. The alternative to you fully understanding your job is having a manager who tells you everything you need to do, but not why you are doing it, and then holds you accountable for results you don't understand. How fulfilling is that job going to be for you? The more you understand, the more rewarding and fulfilling your career will be, regardless of the managers and leaders you encounter.

I also want you to be able to EARN what you want to achieve. For some, it is more money, flexibility, recognition, and/or responsibility. Whatever it is for you, I want to give you the tools to EARN it. One of the differentiators in performing with purpose - you don't make money, you EARN it and know you are contributing to something bigger than you! With this mindset, you move to the abundance mentality Stephen Covey refers to in *The 7 Habits of Highly Effective People*[1], and you have the opportunity to do more. Business owners know what they need to do to make an ethical profit (I'm going to give them the benefit of the doubt here), but often that information isn't filtered down to you. You need to understand how you can both contribute to an ethical profit for the business and share in the earnings. Great employees (or employees who are in the right place at the right time) find business owners who can both explain how they make an ethical profit and want to share their *ethical earnings* with their employees, vendors, and community. Notice the emphasis on ethical earnings.

I want to interject here for a moment and let you know the owner or owners of the business you work for are just people. They've been successful enough to buy or start their company, but they are still people who make decisions based on the feedback and data they receive. So, never feel they do not want to hear from you. You are important to their success. It's how they hear from you that can make a difference and using the EARN method will help you understand how to be heard.

Part of understanding how your job function contributes to the company's profitability is understanding the company's overall goals and how your work helps achieve those goals. Unfortunately, many companies don't analyze their business using the SOAR[2] (Strengths, Opportunities, Aspirations, Results) framework to create a positive, strategic plan that focuses on the best of what the company is capable of achieving. SOAR is a process developed by Jacqueline M. Stavros and Gina Hinrichs that allows you to focus on your strengths, the opportunities you have in your marketspace to do it well, your aspirations as a company, and the results you want to achieve. It is a positive way for companies to focus on what's possible and to actively engage their workforce to be part of the company's strategic plan. I highly recommend you check it out!

As you know, the EARN method is a method that allows you to evaluate your tasks. What you may not know is that it is highly effective with the SOAR process. Don't worry if your company isn't using SOAR. using the EARN method will still help you evaluate your tasks. It's something to consider in the future.

End	• What happens if I stop doing this? • Who will miss it? • Do I really know the end recipient's value of what I am doing? • Do I even know who the end recipient is? • Am I sure they want it? Are they happy with it? • When was the last time I asked them?
Automate	• Can I bring technology to bear on the process? • Can I convert manual steps to automated steps? • Can I remove steps? Can I speed it up? • Do I need to slow it down? • Is there a different way to get it done? Better? Faster? Cheaper?

Reassign	• Does this function really belong here? • Who touches this process upstream (before I get it) and downstream (when I am done with it), and in-between (do I have handoffs along the way or do I collaborate to get it done)? • Can I get someone else to do it better, faster, or cheaper? Outsource? Get a vendor to help? A client? A strategic partner?
Nurture	• What's working well? Who is getting the best result? • Where are the positive results? How can I build on those? • What performance am I getting? • Am I getting the best performance out of the whole system? • Is the function performed by multiple people? Do they all get the same result as far as how long it takes to do, quality, customer satisfaction? • What feedback are employees receiving when they perform well?

It's now time for another exercise. Get out the **Critical Function Worksheet** you created earlier in this chapter. Then, review each of your critical functions against the following questions and document your answers in the **EARN Worksheet** you downloaded at the beginning of the chapter.

STEP 1: Decide what process you want to focus on and write the name of the process in the **Process Name** field.

STEP 2: Write down the steps needed to complete this process in order in the **List steps of the process in order** column.

STEP 3: For each step of the process, answer the questions listed in the **End, Automate, Reassign,** and **Nurture** columns. It will take some research and some discussion to fully answer these questions. This will give you a good guideline as to what may be possible, and a good starting place for discussion with others.

Process Name:	End	Automate	Reassign	Nurture
List the steps of the process in order.	What happens if you Stop doing this?	Describe how this step might be fully or partially automated? How much time and money will it cost?	Who in the value chain, upstream or down, can do this better, faster or cheaper?	If you are stuck with it, have you looked at best practices of how it is performed today. What is the best of the best?

I have seen plenty of things defined as critical that were not even missed when the tasks weren't performed. I also discovered performance of functions that were redundant because they were automated or duplicated, as they were already performed by another department, or overkill because other procedures in areas upstream or downstream negated the necessity of the activity. If the reason you do something is because you've always done it that way, you need to probe deeper and ask why. If you're not sure why you're doing something, ask. If you are performing an unnecessary task because you are worried you won't have a job if you tell your management it isn't necessary, stop and figure out where you can have value first. Most managers like to keep employees who both save them money and alert them when something isn't necessary. To perform with purpose, you need to challenge the status quo appropriately and understand why.

At one point in my career, I worked for an insurance company. I was very excited to be chosen for a special project testing new software for accuracy in claims processing. I was part of a team of six and we worked in a separate room on a three-month project. This meant that every day for eight hours a day we worked on creating test scripts, manipulating claims, and testing the results. We had thousands of examples we needed to test, so as the end of the three months came closer, we realized we would not finish on time. This type of work is monotonous and I hated doing it. However, I loved being part of this special team. So, every morning I put on a smile and made a game out of how many test scripts I could run before I found a bug in the software. Since I was working with a group of conscientious employees, once we discovered we couldn't meet the deadline, we went to management, explained the situation, and offered two solutions: an extension on the time-frame or overtime to complete the project. I was exhausted and disappointed when management elected overtime. We grumbled and wished we had not offered overtime as a solution because we weren't even excited about making extra money. We were too tired to care. We all worked 12-14-hour days, including weekends, to complete the project on time and finished at 6:00 P.M. on the evening of our deadline. We were all burnt out, but extremely proud we finished on time. It was a Friday night, so we went out and celebrated our success (I might have celebrated a little too much) and then went home to crash and burn for the rest of the weekend. The following Monday, I resumed my normal job duties. One week after the project deadline, the Friday after I returned to my normal job duties, I saw the vice president (VP), who was in charge of the project and asked, "Did you like our report?" I hadn't received any feedback on the project and was anxious to know how we did. The VP looked me in the eyes and said, "I haven't had a chance to look at that yet. I'm sure it's fine." And then he walked away. I was crushed. I was angry. I was disappointed and I felt devalued. How would you have felt?

How do you think it would have helped my organization if we had understood who needed the information and why? Could we have made better decisions in giving alternatives? Do you think overtime was a good choice for the organization? Do you think my situation would have turned out differently if I had used the EARN model?

I left that job shortly afterwards and assured them it was nothing they did. I just found a better opportunity. I should have told them the real reason but by then, I had given up. They stole my passion. Do you understand why I was looking for that opportunity?

** A note to business owners and managers: employees who perform with purpose operate under a *don't burn your bridges* mentality. They smile and say it was just too good of an opportunity to pass up. Rest assured, if you provide a learning and growth environment, where employees feel valued and know what they do makes a difference, those other opportunities will never take them away from you!

As an employee, you may often feel you aren't as informed as your supervisor or manager. To put your mind at ease, I want to share an experience I had working with a leadership group of supervisors and managers. We were focusing on teamwork and creating efficiencies, and did an exercise where we went around the table two times at every meeting. The first time, each leader had to ask for help with something they were struggling with that week, and the second time, each leader would offer to help with one of the issues. The reason we did this was to teach the leaders to raise their hand and ask for help.

At the first meeting, we started going around the table and one manager said she was having an issue because costs were way up on her team since she had to repeatedly order and pay $25 for a specific document that never arrived. She had no idea why she had to continually reorder this document when it supposedly had been delivered to the firm. As she described the document and the issues she was facing in her area, a supervisor raised her hand and said, "I'm so sorry. Sam on my team receives those documents. We have never known what to do with them, so she keeps them in a bin on her desk and at the end of every month, we shred them." These two departments were on the same floor and in the same building. Do not assume your supervisor or manager knows more than you. You know the old saying about assume: when you assume something, you take the risk of making an *ass* out of *u* and *me* (*ass u me*). Remember, this was a group of supervisors and managers. If their company had used the EARN method to evaluate the process, Sam would have identified who needed that document before another department created a work-around that cost the company money.

Often times, the reason these issues aren't detected or fixed is because someone else has created the work-around, and they have solved their immediate issue without taking the time to identify the cause of it. The EARN method will help you identify where to dedicate time and resources to create efficiency, and make sure the work you do matters!

To help you start your inquiry process, I created **The Handy Dandy, (and Incomplete) List of Questions**. It is by no means complete and I add to it all the time. So, feel free to send your suggestions to contact@ earnmethodbook.com. I'd love to add your suggestions for others to use, and give you credit of course! Ensure you download a copy of this handout and keep it at your desk as a reminder to ask questions when you're analyzing a task.

The Handy Dandy (and Incomplete) List of Questions

- Why am I doing this?
- Can I live with things as they are, without the change? (Am I living with things as they are already or is this new?)
- Why am I making the change?
- Who is suffering and do they know it?
- How big is this problem? Really? Can you quantify it? I've seen plenty of businesses spend huge amounts of money on inconsequential issues.
- What happens if I don't do anything?
- How many are there? How frequently does it occur?
- Do I need to go backward to fix things, or just forward?
- Does it belong here? (Am I designing the people around the process or the process around the people?)
- Can someone else do it better, faster, or cheaper?
- How much will it cost?
- How much do I stand to lose?
- Who will I piss off?
- Who really needs to know?
- When do they need to know? (Before, during, after)
- How much detail do they need?
- Why am I telling them? (Because they need to know, because I want to get someone in trouble, because I want people to see how smart I am)
- Do I need more opinions or info? From whom?
- Have I asked the right people?
- Do I need permission? From whom? (Do you know your authority?)
- Is it happening too fast? Too slow?
- What happens when I speed it up/slow it down?
- Who is this really helping?
- Has the solution I've come up with solved the problem?
- What new problems may I have created for someone else? (See *Who will I piss off?* above)

- Have you looked at/experienced the process or problem yourself? (Do you know what you're talking about?)
- Has someone shown you the problem?
- Are your sources of information credible? Trust, but verify!
- Is there a temporary solution?
- Is there a compromise solution?
- Is this a simple solution? Have I made it as simple as possible?
- Can I live with minimizing the risk or improvement instead of eliminating it or maximizing it?
- If you are at 0%, would you be better off to go to 50% or 80% if you can't get to 100%?
- Can everyone involved live with the solution? (Doesn't necessarily mean they agree 100%, but will they support it 100%?)

Chapter 1 Positive Impact Points Summary

We've done a lot in this chapter. I figured you were the type who would want to get right to the work and learn what you could do today to perform with purpose. I do want to take a moment now and recap all you've done.

In this chapter, you:

- Wrote a job description for what you do
- Identified the critical functions of your job and completed the Critical Function Worksheet, identifying the documentation and measurements for each function, as well as how you perform
- Identified the training and measurements required for your job and identified what you needed to document to train someone else on how to do the job to achieve the measurements
- Reviewed the EARN method
- Printed the Handy Dandy (and Incomplete) List of Questions to refer to as you continue to evaluate job tasks

If you haven't completed these activities yet, I recommend that you take the time to finish them before moving to chapter 2. Feel free to send any questions you have to contact@earnmethodbook.com.

"Leadership is solving problems. The day soldiers stop bringing you their problems is the day you have stopped leading them. They have either lost confidence that you can help them or concluded that you do not care. Either case is a failure of leadership."
~Colin Powell

CHAPTER 2
Where You Do What You Do

In this chapter, the Positive Impact Points we will review include:

- It's not just your job, it's your life
  - You aren't two people - how you spend your time at work is how you are living
- Being realistic
  - Set goals and expectations you can meet
- Failing Forward
  - Mistakes will help you grow and learn, as long as you use that information to move forward
- Your organization's values and culture
  - Identify the values you see in action and the actual culture of your organization from what you see, not the story posted on posters in the lobby
- Determining the right culture and values fit for you

- Understand how your values and needs from your culture align with your organization's values and culture

The worksheets you'll need include:

- Employment Synergy Assessment
- My Ideal Organizational Culture

You can find worksheets here: www.earnmethodbook.com.

Now, let's get started with what attracted you to the job you currently have.

How did you end up working where you work? What attracted you to the organization? Is this your dream career? Your dream environment? Are you excited and happy to work there? Is it what you expected? Let's be frank, many corporate cultures don't measure up to their own hype.

How do you feel when you work there? Does your boss care about you? Do you feel valued? How do you feel when you leave? Your feelings when you leave work are often what you take home with you to your friends, loved ones, and community. So, if you have a bad day at work, you will likely have a negative mind-set when you get home.

There are several healthy remedies to help you feel better (we won't discuss the unhealthy ones, such as alcohol and drugs): listening to relaxing music, exercising, practicing meditation, deep (diaphragmatic) breathing, or taking a yoga class. And, while I think you should continue doing these healthy remedies (if that's your thing), I suggest you consider the impact of your job on your life. It's not "just a job;" it's how you're living. The following quote is one of my favorites:

How we spend our days is, of course, how we spend our lives. What we do with this hour, and that one, is what we are doing.   —Annie Dillard

---

So, what are you doing? Being happy at your workplace is more than choosing your attitude; it's choosing a culture that's right for you. This was highlighted for me recently when I was talking to a friend of mine who landed her dream job. I'd like to share this story to emphasize the importance of the work you did in chapter 1 because this situation couldn't happen in your organization with the work you just did. Let's take a look.

Chloe was 19, loved animals, and wanted to work with animals to eventually become a veterinary technician. She didn't aspire to be a CEO or buy her own clinic and just wanted to do something she enjoyed, that she felt also contributed to her income and society. She looked at many jobs and even worked part time at some kennels and veterinary offices to be sure she liked the work. She discovered an organization that was hiring and on paper, had everything she was looking for: progressive management, good benefits, tuition reimbursement, a caring environment for pets and their owners, and more. She knew this was the opportunity she prayed she'd find. I told her I was interested to hear more about her new career and this amazing culture, and we talked weekly about her experience. It unfolded like this:

Week One

Chloe woke up early, excited and ready to begin. When she arrived, she was introduced to the staff and then advised to just jump right in and start working. She felt completely overwhelmed, as she was given no special training, no goals, no expectations, and no one for her to shadow. She wasn't sure if she was doing things correctly, and there was no way to measure how she was doing. Occasionally, Chloe's supervisor would give her input —and that usually meant she was doing something wrong. By the end of the week, Chloe was exhausted, anxious, insecure, and grouchy. She retreated to her room to sleep all weekend.

I call this type of learning, *learn by fire!* Although it is highly ineffective and a contributing factor to high turnover, I find that many managers and organizations still use this practice.

Are you seeing the importance of the work you did in chapter 1? Can you imagine how your training documentation could benefit Chloe? How much value would your work bring to this organization right now?

I can only assume this manager learned the same way and has the, *it was good enough for me* mentality. If your chosen organization has this type of training, start asking questions about how your performance is rated and determine how you will have value there. Use what you learned in chapter 1 to discuss with your manager how you can document your learning as you go. Your onboarding and new-hire training are important for quality, efficiency, engagement, and your longevity with the organization. Both you and your organization should take it seriously. If they cannot answer and do not seem receptive to your questions, politely continue on the path they've suggested and immediately begin looking for another opportunity. You are too important to spend your time in an organization that does not care about you!

Week Two

Although Chloe did her best to go back fresh for week two, she started it with an exhaustion hangover. As she continued to flounder, Pat, a long-term employee in another area, began criticizing her work and telling her to do things differently from how Chloe's supervisor had instructed her. She was confused about who to listen to and what she should be doing. Obviously, Chloe was upsetting Pat somehow, but she had no idea how or why. Chloe started feeling that she wasn't suited for the job. She felt isolated, like no one liked her, and like she didn't fit in.

By the end of the week, she was feeling upset and down on herself and wondering why she couldn't seem to do anything right. She went home, watched TV, ignored her friends and family, and spent another weekend sleeping. She was determined she would figure this out, but she was so tired!

Are you seeing the value of the measurements and critical functions you worked on in chapter 1? Can you see how they would have helped Chloe stay focused, understand what she needed to do, and see results as she accomplished learning each task?

Week Three

Chloe woke up on Monday, went through her positive mantras, focused on how she was going to do better, and even did the Wonder Woman stance for confidence. She was going to make this work! Within five minutes of arriving at work, her confidence began to wane.

This week the office had a surprise inspection from a regulatory agency. Being new, she didn't know what needed to be done to prepare for the inspection, but her coworkers and supervisor instructed her to immediately unstack the animal cages. It seemed they routinely stacked the cages one row higher than recommended, so they had to fix this for the inspector. As soon as the inspector left, Chloe was advised to stack the cages back the way they were before. When she asked about the height restrictions, her supervisor told her the regulatory agencies feel it is unsafe and causes stress to the animals, so it's easier to move the cages than to explain why their practices work. Chloe felt uncomfortable restacking the cages and was uncertain if she would be held personally responsible if something bad happened to an animal.

By the end of the week, she was experiencing stomach pain and a headache. She felt like she might be coming down with something, so she spent the weekend at home—sleeping.

Do you think an organization should want you to document practices that go against regulations? If they aren't willing to document what you are required to do, that is another red flag to look for a different opportunity. Make sure you take care of yourself and find another opportunity before you resign. But, if you value integrity, don't work for an organization that does not. Your values need to be aligned with your organization's values for you to have the best work experience.

Week Four

Chloe woke up on Monday both physically and mentally exhausted. It took a lot of energy just to get to work, and she couldn't even muster a full smile. She decided to meet with her supervisor to see if she could make things better. Chloe explained she was getting direction from Pat that differed from what her supervisor had told her, and she had no idea what she was supposed to do. The supervisor waved off her confusion and said, "Oh, Pat. That is just how she is." Chloe also told her supervisor she felt uncomfortable stacking the animal cages higher than they were allowed for an inspection, and again the supervisor waved it off and told her just to do it. The organization knew what it was doing. Chloe walked away from that meeting with the message "Just do whatever anyone tells you, even if you think it is wrong. Don't question; just do." She knew this wasn't going to work.

By the end of the week, Chloe realized she was not going to be happy in this job. Her supervisor would not help her and it was never going to get better. Chloe still had stomach pain, and now she felt she might be coming down with a migraine. She spent the weekend in bed.

Do you think Chloe might feel better if she realized she was in control of what happened next? If she started her new opportunity looking for training documentation, goals, how she would be measured, and what her critical tasks were, then she would have already realized this organization wasn't a fit. She would then be spending her time away from work looking for a different opportunity. The reason Chloe is so sick is that she is taking responsibility for the organization's bad practices and trying to fit in with an organization that doesn't align with her values. Think about the advice you would give Chloe as her friend, knowing what you currently know.

Week Five

Chloe woke up on Monday and told herself, *It's the week before Christmas. I'll look for a job in the new year, and I'll just make this work for now because I need the money. I can do it for a few more weeks.* Finally, she starts to realize she can be in control of her own work life!

When she walked into the veterinarian's office, Chloe mustered the best smile she could and tried to figure out what she should be doing. Then, she overheard Pat telling everyone she was "too sensitive." It appeared that Chloe's supervisor had discussed Chloe's issue with Pat, and now everyone was talking about her. She immediately felt self-conscious, insecure, and isolated. She wondered why no one liked her and why no one could see her side.

The new holiday schedule was released that week and Chloe was scheduled to work on Christmas day from 11:00 A.M. to 6:00 P.M. She was advised there could be no changes. This wasn't a surprise to her since she was new. However, Chloe's family had already told her they would schedule their holiday plans around her shift. All she wanted to do was get through the holiday season and get out of there. Chloe had been spending all of her free time holed up in her apartment and hadn't even decorated, let alone shopped for anyone. She needed to get out of her funk.

By the end of the week, she started resigning herself to the fact that her situation was making her someone she didn't want to be. Her family and friends were tired of her calling them on her way home from work crying and whining about her job. She needed to get through it without dwelling on it every day. One of her friends wanted to call the regulators and report her company. Chloe wondered if she should do that herself.

What do you think? Chloe has finally decided she needs to find another job but look at the effect the last five weeks have had on her health, happiness, and friends and family. I want you to have the tools to leave an organization like this before it has a negative impact on you. An organization is only as good as the employees that work there, and this type of organization doesn't deserve someone as talented and conscientious as you!

Week 6

It was Christmas Eve. Chloe woke up late and used every ounce of effort she had to pull herself out of bed to get ready and go to work. Even though she knew she was going to resign, she still started every morning hopeful that something would be better, and she left every day disappointed that nothing was. After she left work that day at 2:00 P.M., her supervisor called to tell her she must now come in at 7:00 A.M. on Christmas day and work until 4:00 P.M. Chloe started crying. She explained that her family and friends had created all their plans around her work schedule. Some of them were traveling and they were expecting her to be there in the morning. It was too late to change their plans and she wanted to be with them. She was told there was no way to change a holiday shift, but now hers was being changed. The supervisor listened and replied uncaringly, "I'm sorry. There is nothing I can do. You need to be here at 7:00 A.M. tomorrow."

Chloe resigned. When she called her family, they told her enough was enough and advised her they would help her until she found another opportunity. They also told her story to everyone they came in contact with for the next several months, which is not the word-of-mouth advertising any organization wants. Her resigning cost the company not only her salary, but an abandoned shift on Christmas day, and the cost of hiring and training her replacement (well, maybe just hiring since they don't really train new employees). The estimated cost of replacing an employee is 1.5 times the employee's salary; but in many cases, it is more. There is also a cost to negative word-of-mouth advertising, company clients witnessing high employee turnover, and the negative footprints it leaves in your culture. I'm not suggesting you share this information with your organization; I just want you to know it. It is a lose/lose situation for you and for your organization if you resign in the first year. And I want you to consider this as we talk about your interview process and finding the right fit for you.

The Encore

I chose this story because it has an encore. Since Chloe resigned and did not work her last shift, her supervisor informed her that she was reducing her salary for the hours she had already worked as punishment for resigning without notice. Since your company is not allowed to reduce your salary without notifying you in advance of doing the work, I helped her write a letter to the owner of the company explaining what happened. The owner mailed her a check for what he owed her. ***Period.*** He did not ask a single question, find out what happened, or ask her why she resigned. I told Chloe that meant the culture was acceptable to the owner.

I'd like to stop here and suggest that if this happens to you, let it go. You are not going to change the owner's practices, and the owner has the right to run their business as they choose. I am focused on you finding the right culture for you and focusing on previous bad experiences will not help you get there. Take a deep breath, realize it is a learning experience, and plan for your next opportunity. I like to refer to this as *failing forward*.

So how can you know in advance what a company's culture is like? One way is observation and asking behavioral questions in your interview. Have you ever heard of a dad offering this advice to his daughter? "Pay attention to how a man treats his mother because that's likely how he'll treat you." In that same light, how an organization treats their customers and employees is a good indication of how closely they follow the rhetoric they put on paper, or in their marketing and advertising. Remember, ***how you do anything is how you do everything.*** Paying attention to these things is key. Do your due diligence to ensure you find the right fit.

To help you define what to look for in a company's culture, we created an assessment for you to evaluate your values and determine what is important to you. Use the results to either compare your values to the culture you are in right now or create questions to learn more about a company's culture in an interview. This is not a scientifically proven method and no animals were harmed in the production of these questions. In fact, there are no right or wrong answers; it is just about you and what is important to you. You won't find a chart at the end that states, "If you chose these answers, you are more likely to..." This is just a way for you to consider what is important to you, what your organization values, and if you and your organization (or potential future organization) align.

Open the **Employment Synergy Assessment** you downloaded at the beginning of this chapter and see what you find!

STEP 1: Take some time to read over the different types of cultures and think about what is important to you, what you like, and how you thrive.

STEP 2: In the **Organization** and **Me** columns, rate each type of culture on a scale of 1 to 6; 1 being not important and 6 being extremely important.

STEP 3: Then, in the **Difference** column, record the difference between the two categories, and look for instances where you find greater than a two-point difference.

Culture is:	Organization	Me	Difference
Organization or CEO focused – the organization talks a lot about increasing shareholder value and focuses mainly on gaining awards and CEO recognition	1 2 3 4 5 6	1 2 3 4 5 6	
Customer focused – the organization has signs on the wall that state the customer is ALWAYS right and talks about the number one priority being the customer	1 2 3 4 5 6	1 2 3 4 5 6	

Culture is:	Organization	Me	Difference
Employee focused – The organization has a strong Learning and Development department and has opportunities in place for you to learn new skills, advance and measure your success	1 2 3 4 5 6	1 2 3 4 5 6	
Family Oriented – the employees refer to each other as one big happy family	1 2 3 4 5 6	1 2 3 4 5 6	
Focused on Individual Contributors – The organization is focused on individual production and what you contribute individually to the team	1 2 3 4 5 6	1 2 3 4 5 6	
Focused on Teamwork – There is a culture of working collaboratively and using shared spaces	1 2 3 4 5 6	1 2 3 4 5 6	
Competitive – Being the best is important and people thrive when they are pushing each other to be even better	1 2 3 4 5 6	1 2 3 4 5 6	

Culture is:	Organization	Me	Difference
Stable – The culture has a deep history and prides itself on continuing to stick to its roots and offer the customer a familiar experience every time – they still have paper forms	1 2 3 4 5 6	1 2 3 4 5 6	
Growing – It seems like every single week there is a new hire orientation class and you are doubling and tripling the number of employees	1 2 3 4 5 6	1 2 3 4 5 6	
Structured – There are processes and procedures in place for every aspect of everyone's job and everyone is expected to follow them	1 2 3 4 5 6	1 2 3 4 5 6	
Honest – Integrity is woven into the fabric of the culture and it is important to always do the right thing, even if the organization loses money as a result	1 2 3 4 5 6	1 2 3 4 5 6	

Culture is:	Organization						Me						Difference
Creative – Innovation is important to the culture and they work to hear new ideas, create new projects or business lines and continually improve and grow	1	2	3	4	5	6	1	2	3	4	5	6	
Compassionate – they care about the welfare of all including the community and all stakeholders	1	2	3	4	5	6	1	2	3	4	5	6	
Exciting – Every day the employees are breaking new ground with discoveries, ideas or projects	1	2	3	4	5	6	1	2	3	4	5	6	
Technically Savvy – Technology is important, and the organization is using cutting edge technology	1	2	3	4	5	6	1	2	3	4	5	6	
Scholarly – Learning is important in this culture and they talk a lot about skills and knowledge, succession planning and promoting from within	1	2	3	4	5	6	1	2	3	4	5	6	

How does it feel to focus on what's important to you? Have you considered finding the right cultural fit before now? If not, do you think this could help you find an organization where you both fit in and feel happy? Your answers will help you focus on what that best culture fit is for you. There is no right culture, but there certainly is a right culture fit. You may want to probe a little deeper in areas that are important to you, or where you recorded more than a two-point difference. If you are interviewing and have a chance to talk to more than one person at a company or in a department, compare their answers and see if they are aligned in their perception of the organization and its culture.

Many people just sit tight, accept where they are, and put up with it – it's a job. If that's you, make sure it is not affecting your life, relationships, or how you show up in your community. If it's not, then keep doing what you're doing. Either way, I hope you'll take some of these ideas and start making small, incremental improvements in your job. Fear is a great deterrent to change. I know plenty of people who want to do things differently or pursue a different career path, but they also worry about keeping a roof over their head and food on the table. Those are important things to consider. For those of you who have children, I ask you to consider what you are teaching your child(ren) about work. If you dread Monday, praise hump day, celebrate Friday, and pray for Saturday, then your child(ren) learn that's normal.

If you look at successful franchises, let's take sports for example, their success is clearly linked to the culture they set and the alignment of their leadership, management, and players toward shared values and goals. Any weakness in that chain can thwart success. How can one coach fail and another succeed with the same players? How about a player who underperforms on one team and blossoms with another? The inverse is also possible. The alignment between ownership, management, and employees is critical to organizational success. You matter and are just as important in the equation as anyone else. In football, a brilliant owner with a star quarterback does not win games if there is no one to catch the ball! Everyone on the team is important to winning the game.

I have seen businesses and teams rise and fall as these ingredients shift. Pay attention to this alignment in your current situation, and if it isn't meeting your needs, consider having a conversation with your manager or searching for a new opportunity that does. Depending on how your company is structured, sometimes you only need to move to a different department. Look for what works for you.

The first corporate job I ever had was in a mortgage company. I worked on a team assigned to work properties in default (where the property owner hadn't paid) by the terminal digit of the loan number. Each property had all the pertinent property information put into a file, and each file was assigned a number. This meant someone worked all files ending in 1, someone else handled the 2s, and so on. We communicated with vendors, attorneys, and governmental agencies on each file we were assigned. I noticed on the second or third day on the job how each team member was constantly crossing over with communication. I would hang up with an attorney in one state and five minutes later, I would hear a coworker calling that same office I just talked to on a different file. I suggested to my supervisor that it might be a good idea to assign files by region or state, rather than by the terminal digits. She told me, "We have always done it this way and it is good enough." Eventually, the volume increased and we added more staff to keep up. So, I renewed my suggestion to regionalize the workflow and had the opportunity to discuss it with my manager and the VP of our area. The manager was still dead set against it, but I could see that the VP thought it had merit. Unfortunately, he was unwilling to require the manager to make any changes (that should have been a hint for me, but I was still young and very optimistic). The manager had been with the organization for nearly 12 years. I knew she wasn't going to budge and the VP wasn't either because the results were "good enough" and "we have always done it this way." So, I had an idea; not a great one, but an idea. I typed up (yes typed - this was in the days before PCs and email, which shows you how old I am) a very flattering resume for my manager and mailed it anonymously to four competitors in our area. I am not suggesting in any way that you should ever do anything like this, I'm just sharing with you some of the bad decisions I made along the way. Three weeks later, the manager pulled us into a meeting, told us that she had accepted a position at another company and would be leaving. I heard through the grapevine that she was recruited by our competitor and she was getting a significant pay increase. Yes, that decision lacked integrity, and as I've said, I would not make the same choice today. I want you to both understand the outcome, and why you wouldn't want to do something like this. I'm not perfect and I've made a lot of mistakes. After my manager left, I got promoted and regionalized the department. Efficiency went up, our vendors and attorneys were happy, our capacity increased, and the VP looked like a genius. Sometimes things work out for everybody – temporarily at least.

I ended up leaving 18 months later because I could not influence the overall culture. "Good enough" is very hard to change. I took a job at a startup mortgage company, where I knew I could help *create* the culture I was seeking. As Kenny Roger's says in his famous song, The Gambler, "You gotta know when to hold 'em, know when to fold 'em, know when to walk away, and know when to run …" You try to make changes where you can but sometimes, it is just time to move on.

Some companies have excellent management structures and others simply suck. Most of the time, companies suck because their leadership allows it. Every behavior you see in a business, good or bad, exists because someone or something reinforces it. Finding the courage to initiate change within your workplace, or to move on to another, is a tough decision. If you are going to fail, fail fast so you can cut your losses and move on to something better – remember fail *forward*! You do have a choice. If you choose to speak up, you will need, passion, patience, persistence, and most importantly, a great willingness to listen and seek common ground. You deserve to go home from your job every day feeling valued, excited, and good about what you do. Check your energy levels. If you are exhausted, your body is sending you a red flag. Remember, this is your life and your happiness should matter to *you*!

It's time to take out the **My Ideal Organizational Culture Worksheet** that you downloaded at the beginning of this chapter and focus on what is the most important for you. You do not have to share this information; it is just for you. So, take some time to reflect and have fun with this exercise. If you have any questions, feel free to email us at contact@earnmethodbook.com.

Chapter 2 Positive Impact Points Summary

This chapter gave you the opportunity to explore what type of culture you need to really enjoy your work and perform with purpose.

In this chapter, you:

- Acknowledged that this isn't just your job, it's your life
- Identified your organization's values and culture
- Determined the right culture and values fit for you
- Documented what you need to be valued at work

If you haven't completed these activities yet, I recommend that you take the time to finish them before moving to chapter 3. Feel free to send any questions you have to contact@earanmethodbook.com.

"Good is the enemy of great. And that is one of the key reasons why we have so little that becomes great. We don't have great schools, principally because we have good schools. We don't have great government, principally because we have good government. Few people attain great lives, in large part because it is just so easy to settle for a good life."   *~ James C. Collins*

CHAPTER 3
How Do You Communicate?

In this chapter, the Positive Impact Points we will review include:

- Dropping the sarcasm
  - The language you choose can have a profound effect on how others hear you
- Asking questions
  - Allows you to listen and allows the other person to feel heard
- Using positive, present-tense language
  - Using present-tense verbs makes your communication clear and easily understood
- Being specific
  - Say exactly what you mean
- Using EARN to identify opportunities

- The EARN method is a great tool to identify if there is something that can *end, automate, reassign,* or *nurture*

The worksheets you'll need include:

- Your Communication Skills Worksheet
- Positive Present-Tense Language Worksheet

You can find worksheets here: www.earnmethodbook.com.

Now let's get started looking at how you communicate.

Your communication skills are important in this process. EARN allows you to identify opportunities, but you need to be able to communicate your findings. There are a lot of effective tools and resources out there for you to work on and improve how you communicate. I suggest you explore these products if you feel like you have issues communicating. I will share some communication tips with you, but if you are struggling, you'll want to seek additional resources.

Let's start by completing the **Your Communication Skills Worksheet** you downloaded in the beginning of this chapter. Review the instructions in the worksheet, answer the questions, and when you're ready, come back here to continue.

Your Communication Skills

> *I want you to think about when and where you communicate effectively to see if you can identify situations or people that can help you communicate more effectively in other areas of your life.*
>
> Think about when and where you communicate effectively to identify situations or people that can help you communicate more effectively in other areas of your life. For example, think of a good conversation you had with someone when you were sharing information, listening, and responding to what they had to say. This could be a simple conflict, for

example having a conversation with your roommate about cleaning the kitchen and exploring what works for them, or it could be talking to a friend about taking a trip. Think of a successful conversation where you walked away feeling you were glad you had the conversation and felt you communicated well. This is from your perspective, so unless the other person has shared with you that they did not feel you communicated well, if you felt you did, choose that conversation. Do you have a conversation in mind? It can be anything, and I'd prefer it be recent, but if you can only think of a conversation that occurred a while ago, that works too. Have one?

Excellent, now answer the following questions based on that conversation:

- What did you do well in this conversation?
- What about this conversation worked well or flowed?
- Where have you used these same skills in other conversations you've had?

What did you discover about your strengths in this exercise? Were you able to identify what allows you to be effective when listening and responding? Think about what's effective for you. I have been studying, training, and reading about communication for years and I still work at it every day. I'll share with you some insight into my successes and ask that you to start looking at your own. I am a huge Brené Brown fan, and if you are interested in learning about courageous conversations, I recommend *Dare to Lead*. She's very authentic and carries a punch, so I only recommend her to people who are really interested in learning more about themselves.

The first tip I want to share with you is to drop the sarcasm. Brené takes a deeper dive into this in her work, but I want to share with you my own experiences and how doing this had a positive impact for me. If you occasionally make snide comments, crack funny side jokes or are known for your sarcastic remarks, consider leaving them at home when you go to work. Yes, I want you to bring your whole self to work but let me share a little about sarcasm – many people don't like it!

I grew up in a family where dry humor and sarcasm was the main form of communication. It was witty, considered funny and just the way we communicated. When I entered my first job, I was surprised by how sensitive and offended people were by my humor. I was only kidding. I continued to have some difficult conversations with my peers and leaders about how others perceived my sarcasm, but I still didn't understand the impact it was having on my career until I started working as a trainer in a big law firm. Although I was sarcastic, I was also extremely optimistic and often referred to as Smiley or Pollyanna by those close to me. I really enjoyed my job as a trainer, and I had a boss that I admired and respected. When I had my first performance review, my boss rated me low on the value of being positive. I remember sitting across from her, open-mouthed and saying, "You don't think I'm positive?" Notice how I worded the question. She replied, "No, I don't. You make negative comments and you need to look for the positive in situations instead of pointing out what people are doing wrong." Talk about a reality check! I thought I was bubbly, happy, smiley, and positive, and she saw me as negative and a Debbie Downer. I admit I went through all the normal stages of denial after that conversation, saying she didn't know what she was talking about, asking my friends and neighbors to validate that I didn't act that way, looking for other job opportunities, and so on. But, at the end of the day, I knew that there was some truth in what she was saying and had encountered issues with sarcasm before. So, I decided to take a look at how I was communicating and start working on dropping the sarcasm.

Another important thing I have learned about sarcasm is that people who learn English as a second language have a difficult time interpreting and understanding sarcasm. It is not an effective form of communication. Your best practice is not to use sarcasm, and if it is natural for you to use sarcasm, you'll have to work on this one. I'll share with you how I was able to start working on it, and still do today with my second tip.

My second tip is asking questions, not just any type of question, but conditionally positive questions. Ask people to tell you what is going right for them today. You'll find you bring a smile to their face and learn a lot of interesting information while you are creating great connections. Ask others about their day, their weekend, an object they are carrying, a picture on their desk, etc., and then wait for their response. This is what I did and when I focused on asking questions, I was able to listen more and work on not giving sarcastic answers. I focused on this every day and by the end of the first month, my boss met with me and said she had never seen such a dramatic turn-around. Meanwhile, the only thing I had changed in my behavior was asking questions. She was proud of my positive attitude and appreciated me taking it seriously and living by our company values. Seeing that asking questions was working, I began studying more about inquiry and how to ask better questions. That's when I learned about appreciative inquiry and improv. I will touch on them briefly, but if you are interested in deeper learning, I recommend checking them out.

Attending a local improv group is both fun and very helpful in communication, teaching you how to communicate in the moment, learning more about your initial responses, training you to think quick on your feet, and learning the power of using "Yes, and…" instead of "but." The most helpful framework I've used is Appreciate Inquiry, which is a positive approach to change management. It is also a way to use questions and curiosity to look for the best of what is. Many of you may have heard the saying, "You find what you are looking for." Appreciative Inquiry helps you look for the positive using questions like, "What's the best thing that's happened to you today? What do you like best about my communication style?" and "Where have I performed the best in the last week?" Focusing on the positive allows everyone to learn more about what's working and focuses on what we want instead of what we don't want. I also find it gives you the opportunity to talk about what you are doing well and get positive feedback for doing a great job. Managers are taught to give praise and positive feedback to their employees; help them know what you deserve praise and feedback for doing.

One of the reasons I wanted to write this book for employees is because I want you to understand what your manager does, what they are held responsible for doing, and what they are learning. When your behavior and communication align with what your manager wants and needs, everybody wins. You just want to communicate it in a way that is respectful and effective, and conditionally positive questions are a great tool to do this. Imagine saying this to your manager, "I worked really hard on my last project and I want to make sure your needs were met. Can you tell me what you think the best result from the project is and where my hard work was most effective?" Your manager will start thinking of an answer, and when they start thinking, they are going to be thinking about the best work you contributed.

My next tip is to use positive, present-tense language. This means using present tense verbs focusing on what is possible. For example, if a coworker sends you an email and asks you to have lunch on Friday, instead of responding, "I can't. I have a meeting during lunch on Friday." Reply instead with something like this: "I am free for lunch on Thursday (1/1) or next Wednesday (1/5)." This effectively communicates you cannot have lunch Friday but tells your coworker what options are available. This is going to be effective when you work with your team, talk to your clients, and meet with your manager. Let's say you want to meet with your manager to talk about your critical functions. You show your manager the critical functions worksheet you are working on and ask what else should be included. Your manager gets excited about the work you are doing and says, "I want you to document everything you do. Can you have that done by next Friday so I can take it to the executive board meeting?" The reality is that you cannot document the information by next Friday. You barely have time to get your regular job done, let alone spend time documenting what you do. So, how do you respond?

Let's think about this. If we're looking for what's possible, what can we identify? Maybe you have time to work on the documentation if someone else performs your job duties for you one day? Maybe you have some free time this weekend and would be willing to work on it if your boss approves overtime? Maybe someone else can sit with you and document what you do while you are performing your job? What possibilities can you think of in your organization? Think about what's possible, and then tell your boss using positive, present-tense language. Maybe you respond by saying, "I can have an outline of the procedures and a time-frame for how long it will take me to document them by next Friday." This response is letting your boss know what you can reasonably do without saying no or being negative.

In contrast, if you respond to your manager's request by saying, "I can't do it by Friday." You don't indicate when you can have it done, or what options are available. Your manager would not understand what other deadlines you have, if you are planning on taking a vacation day, or if you just don't want to do it. He or she wouldn't have enough information from your response to effectively help you. Do you think it would be more effective to say, "I have to finish the XYZ Report by Friday and I anticipate that will take another 10 hours. Would you prefer I move the deadline for the XYZ Report to next

Thursday and have this assignment done by Friday, or do both the XYZ Report and this project have to be done by next Thursday?" This allows you and your manager to have a productive conversation that begins with possibilities instead of you saying no. I know I like it much better when I'm given options instead of being told what can't be done.

Try rewriting a few negative responses yourself using the **Positive Present-Tense Language Practice Worksheet** that you downloaded at the beginning of this chapter.

What did you notice while you were practicing? Did you start to respond with what you cannot do? Responding with the possibilities allows the other person to respond more effectively.

Let's look at another scenario. You're on a tight schedule and you stop at a local sandwich shop to order lunch. You look at the menu and say, "I'll take the Reuben." The server says, "I'm sorry, we can't make Reubens today." You respond, "Okay, then I'll take the Limburger Rye Bread Sandwich," to which the server replies, "We can't make that one either." Can you feel the frustration beginning? The reason the sandwich shop can't make the sandwiches is because they are currently out of rye bread. It would be more effective if the server responded to the initial request for the Reuben with: "I'm sorry we don't have any rye bread today. We can make your sandwich on wheat bread, or you can choose any sandwich made with wheat, white, or sourdough bread."

That leads me to my last tip - be specific. When you are communicating what you can do and when, be very specific about what you are going to do and the exact date and time it will be done. If you tell your boss you can get that report to them next Tuesday, be specific about when next Tuesday. Is it Tuesday morning? Afternoon? End of Day? The more specific you are, the more effective your communication is.

I've had people tell me communicating this way makes their boss uncomfortable, or challenges people. If you feel that way, consider what is uncomfortable or challenging. If you ask a question with the desire to know if the possibility you are requesting is an option, you will be both effective and nonconfrontational. As you do the work in this book, it is important that you are able to ask your manager questions and discuss possibilities.

If your manager isn't receptive to you asking respectful, specific questions, consider other factors, such as the tone of your voice, your body language, or your history. Most often, managers appreciate having enough information to effectively provide direction.

Let's go back to our grocery store scenario and talk about how to apply this same concept of looking for opportunities using the EARN method.

You're at work and you repeatedly see small children grab things placed in the bottom of the checkout line, making it tough for their parents to wait in line. Instead of just thinking that you need to move the rack, you apply the EARN method and think, what could you *end, automate, reassign,* or *nurture?* Maybe you think about reassigning and want to suggest to your manager that the store remove the items on the bottom rack and replace them with a TV monitor that shows cartoons. That way, the children would be occupied and the adults would have an easier time checking out.

How would you talk to your manager about this idea? Would you start with the problem, talking about the kids crying in line, or would you start with the opportunity? Maybe you'd say, "I've been thinking about the opportunities for impulse buys in the checkout lines and would like to talk to you about an idea I have to increase the sales." Remember, you are a cashier and perform with purpose. "Children are drawn to what is at their current eye-level, so I wonder what would happen if we had one lane with a TV monitor that plays a cartoon-like show geared toward children? Then, the children would be entertained in line and the parents would have the opportunity to look at the impulse buys geared to them on the top of the racks." You could continue with your idea of what to show on the TV monitor; perhaps you want to create a show in-house or partner with a local PBS station? Do you see how presenting your ideas as possibilities with a positive outcome, instead of focusing on the problem, gives you more time to talk about your good idea? If you start with the issues with the children in line, your manager may want to help you solve that problem, which would not give you the opportunity to talk about your idea. Be specific and focus on what you want.

I remember an incident when I worked in a call center. I don't know if you've ever worked in a call center, but a typical goal is to answer every call that comes in within 30 seconds. Our call wait time was over four minutes. A conscientious employee came to me and told me they thought we needed more people to answer the phones. He explained that everyone was working as hard as they could, but there was no way to keep up with the number of calls we were receiving. The employee went on to explain that every day someone was either out sick or on vacation, so we needed enough employees on staff to allow for the shortage. The employee stated he was very stressed, as was everyone around him, and if we didn't get more people, some people would quit, and the problem would be even worse.

I stopped the employee right there and asked what the possibilities were. The employee was so focused on the problem, he hadn't really thought about any potential solutions, except adding more employees. I asked the employee to stop and use the EARN Method. We knew the average wait time for incoming calls was four minutes, and that every day the staff is at least one employee short due to vacation or illness. Looking at **nurture**, what do you think I asked next to identify the opportunity? Good. I asked if they had ever answered the calls within 30 seconds. The employee stated they had, so we talked about what the conditions were and what had changed. We looked at the data log to see why the customers were calling and what they needed. Through this process, we identified we had made a change in our process, which was causing the customers to call.

The employee focused on the change in the process and suggested we create a focus group of employees and customers and change the process again. I thought it was a great idea and we did just that. As a result, the number of calls we received dropped dramatically. The employee was right. We did have more calls coming in than we had staff to handle but adding more staff would not have fixed the problem. The goal is to always look for what's possible.

Some people just do this naturally. I remember one day I was talking to an incredibly gifted developer I worked with and explained that we were having a hard time getting enough employees to work on a special project for a client. The client needed us to help them convert their old system to a new one. The new system did not offer data conversion, so this required us to go into one screen in their old system and then manually key all of the information into their new system. Looking for what was possible, the developer asked me to show him specifically what information I needed to transfer and wanted to see the screen in the current system. He didn't ask for my thoughts; he asked to see the screen. Then, he asked to see the new system and the screen on to which we were manually keying the information. After he had the facts, he used **automate** from the EARN Method, did a quick search, and found a free data conversion program. He came back and said, "You are manually entering all the data from one system to another. I wonder what might happen if you downloaded an app to extract the data? What do you think?" I thought it was a great idea and was able to finish the entire project in one day with one employee.

The process of looking for opportunities is simple, but it takes a lot of work to get proficient. You have to work to retrain your brain to look for opportunities instead of focusing on problems, and the best way to practice is to use it every day. We have been taught since we were very young to look for what's broken and fix it. Research has shown that the more you do this, the more broken things you will find because you see what you are looking for. Start by looking for what's possible and pay attention to what you find. When you are at home, look for what's working. When you're shopping with a friend or working on your hobby, notice what's working well and what you are enjoying. At work, pay attention to how you respond and the information you are sharing with your manager and customers. It takes time, but the more you practice, the more you'll find yourself noticing what's working and what's possible.

Chapter 3: Positive Impact Points Summary

In this chapter, you focused on your communication and learned some tips and techniques to help you focus on positive communication.

You also learned to:

- Focus on dropping the sarcasm
- Start your conversations asking questions
- Use positive, present-tense language
- Be specific
- Use EARN to identify opportunities

If you want to do deeper work with your communication style or how others perceive you, there are some excellent tools out there to explore. Feel free to email me for some of my favorites at contact@earnmethodbook.com.

If you haven't completed these activities yet, I recommend that you take the time to finish them before moving to chapter 4. Feel free to send any questions you have to contact@earnmethodbook.com.

In every day, there are 1,440 minutes. That means we have 1,440 daily opportunities to make a positive impact.   *~Les Brown*

CHAPTER 4

Who You Impact

In this chapter, the Positive Impact Points we will review include:

- The importance of your critical relationships
    - Identifying who you need and who relies on you to do your job effectively
- Areas to make critical relationships even better
    - Reviewing the needs and opportunities for those relationships over the next 18 months
- The impact on others as you perform your duties
    - Reviewing the needs of others and how work gets accomplished
- The importance of treating your vendors like customers
    - Treating your vendors like customers ensures you understand their value
- Understanding relationships are yours to manage
    - Managing your relationships every day with your customers, vendors, coworkers and managers

The worksheets you'll need include:

- My Biggest Accomplishment
- Critical Relationship Worksheet

You can find worksheets here: www.earnmethodbook.com.

Now, let's get started reviewing what you do and how to seek opportunities within it. Who do you do your job for and with? Relationships in business, like in life, often define your success or failure, and employees who perform with purpose are aware of their relationships with others. I'm sure your mother always warned you about hanging around with the wrong crowd, that your friends are a reflection of you, and so on. Many times, we work like we are on an island, blinders on, doing what we get paid to do. Have you ever been frustrated when someone you are working with hands you the "just doing my job" line when you ask them to consider other possibilities?

We don't work in a vacuum; everything we do has an impact on someone. Whatever we do has to keep our ultimate customer in mind. After all, without them we don't get a paycheck. But there are many others that interact with us that play an important role in what our customer experiences.

Consider all the constituents that make your business do what it does, and impact what you do. As I said, our customers are important; all of them. You have obvious external customers that consume and receive a benefit from your actions, and you also have internal customers that you serve. Vendors, suppliers, and service providers are also critical to your work, as are referral sources and other strategic partners who align themselves with your organization.

I am a firm believer that you should treat your constituents like partners, not adversaries. Thinking win/lose (I win, so therefore you must lose) does not foster trust or loyalty. Always put yourself in the shoes of those you impact and seek opportunities that are not only good for you, but good for the whole system.

What does this mean? It means that all relationships are important to your business, not just customers. Before you work on the next activity, think about how important your vendors are to your business. Have you printed anything today? If so, think about how you were able to do that. A vendor either rented or sold you the printer and that same vendor or another vendor provides the ink. Is your printer on a network? If so, do you have an IT department, or do you have a vendor come and help you? How about shipping? A mailroom? This is another area where your feedback is critical because often times you are the one managing these critical relationships. If you don't know the answers to any of these questions, you won't be able to make good decisions at work. How can you act like a business owner if you don't understand the expenses of the business?

I did an exercise in a workshop where they asked me to think of the biggest accomplishment I ever achieved by myself, without anyone's help. Some people in my group said they earned a degree or certification, but the instructor was quick to point out that they had the help of their professors, the school, and the community.

Can you think of something you've achieved without the help of anyone else?

Open the **My Biggest Accomplishment** worksheet you downloaded at the beginning of this chapter and answer the following questions:

- What is your biggest accomplishment so far in your life?
- Who helped you achieve it? Remember, it can be any resource, not just a person (a book, a Google search, a blog, and so on).

I've only heard one answer that may qualify and that is someone who thought of an idea. It's debatable because it was influenced by their life experiences.

Thinking about others helping us moves us into our next exercise, which is identifying the critical relationships that help us accomplish things at work. Our relationships with others are very important to getting our job done. Going back to our grocery store example, I can think of many critical relationships that each cashier would have. Each cashier would have a relationship with their manager, other cashiers, repeat customers, their information technology (IT) department, their trainers, vendors, and so on.

Critical Relationship			
Relationship Name	Internal/ External	Top Three Reasons Why the Relationship is Important	Top Three Relationship Needs/ Opportunities (in the next 18 months)
Jensen's Grocery Store Machine Service	E	1. Service the cash registers 2. Fix any broken cash registers 3. Update bar codes	1. Allow employees to update bar codes in the system 2. Cashiers having a face-to-face meeting with the vendor representative 3. Email receipt option

This worksheet shows relationships and opportunities available for mutual benefit. In this example, the cash register vendor may be very important to the business. How might it help to have the cashiers and the vendors meet quarterly and discuss how the cashiers are using the machines, and what's working well for them?

In another example, if you are in the Accounting department, you may list something as simple as your banking relationship. That relationship is critical because it provides a means for you to conduct commerce. Are you maximizing the relationship? Do they offer electronic statements you can import for ease in reconciliation? Are there special services for businesses to prevent fraud? Remote deposits? Overnight sweep accounts? How about fees and interest rates? Have you evaluated your relationship recently? Do they understand what you do and what your needs are? Have you applied the EARN Method? These teams must work together to get invoices out and cash in. By asking your counterparts to evaluate the relationship too, you may discover opportunities to streamline activities, speed up cash flow, and improve customer satisfaction.

I want you to think about the different relationships you have in your job – the people you rely on to get things done. This could be your postal carrier or UPS service, it could be your computer equipment, phone, office supply vendor, coworkers, lawyers, nurses, and so on.

For this assignment, complete the **Critical Relationships Worksheet** you downloaded at the beginning of this chapter. Identify your important relationships, as well as the needs and opportunities surrounding those relationships. Think in terms of a conscious capitalist (someone who considers the needs of customers, co-workers, investors/owners, suppliers, the community, and the environment)[3]. Remember, who you are at work is who you are.

STEP 1: In the **Relationship Name** column, list the names of all the critical relationships (internal and external) that affect your job, or that you affect from the performance of your duties. I guarantee that if you take some time to reflect, you will be amazed by the number of relationships you rely upon, or rely upon you to perform your job.

STEP 2: In the **Internal/External** column, specify if the relationship is internal or external to your company.

STEP 3: In the next column, define what is important about the relationship. Do you rely on it? Does it rely on you? What happens when everything is clicking? What makes it important? Try to come up with the top three reasons the relationship is important for you. If you can't think of three, just write down one or two. The idea is to really explore why this relationship is important.

STEP 4: In the last column, define how you might seek the opportunity to make this relationship the best it can be in the next 18 months. If it's easier, you can think about it over the next year. I just want you to think about what is going to nurture this relationship over time. What does it look like when everything is optimized? Are there things that can be addressed to enhance the mutual success of this relationship?

Still focusing on accounting, an internal example may be the relationship with a team that performs and bills for a service or product. In a professional service firm, professionals must provide time and billing information for the accounting group to invoice.

To illustrate how this can help you in your job, I'll share a story about what happened with my friend, Frank. He worked on the Implementation team for a communication company. They were having an issue with the Sales and Implementation teams working together to get a new client set up on their system. The Sales team would go out and sell services, but then the Implementation team wasn't able to set the client up for services because they needed more information. Frank decided this wasn't a big deal. He just needed to ask the Sales people to get the information the Implementation team needed, since they had the relationship with the client. I mean, they all worked for the same company and wanted the same thing, right? Which was happy customers implemented on their software. When Frank asked the Sales person to get the information, Frank quickly realized that they all didn't want the same thing. The sales person wanted to sell services and once they sold the services, they needed to spend their time selling the next one, not taking time to service the one they already sold because they got paid for the number of clients sold, not implemented. The sales people were actually paid even if the client was never implemented. Frank's job was to implement the client and he wasn't able to do it without leveraging the Sales person's relationship. What's the opportunity here?

Using *reassign* from the EARN Method, Frank talked to his boss about where the checklist for implementation really belonged. The Sales team was a critical relationship for his team and the Sales team relationship with the client was also a critical relationship. They approached the situation in a new way: *How might it work if we revise the process and ask the Sales people to get the pertinent information up front, compensating them for the extra time by rewarding the teams who implemented the most clients on the system?* Both teams then understood how to work together to accomplish their goal and they were able to perform with purpose.

As people like you continue to step up and take charge of your own destiny, companies will continue to revise their policies and procedures to work for all critical relationships. People want to feel valued in a relationship; like they matter. Treating people like you would treat yourself is a good mantra to follow, unless you're a martyr, then it isn't. Identifying your constituents' wants and needs, delivering them, and sharing your wants and needs will help you forge long-lasting relationships that will endure business cycle fluctuations.

I remember a CFO (Chief Financial Officer) once who was horrible I only saw him once a month when he had a meeting to lash out at everyone over the financial results. He was very short-sighted and didn't look at critical relationships, critical functions, or any metrics besides the financial report, which you probably already know doesn't provide enough information to seek opportunities. Once I figured out that all of his fuel came from one source, I was able to start marrying performance data with financial data to show we needed to focus our attention on more than the bottom-line. I understood critical relationships and the CEO (Chief Executive Officer) and COO (Chief Operations Officer) supported that. The CFO left as soon as he realized the monthly beating approach wasn't going to work. Our running joke about this CFO was that whenever we brought him actual data, he would say, "That can't be right." I'd be surprised if he is still employed at all. Organizations can't afford short-sighted employees. They do too much damage to the culture.

What organizations need are employees who not only look for opportunities, but ones who will turn them into meaningful goals. I will talk about how to do this and how to share this information to make meaningful, profitable change in your organization. You don't have to be an executive to initiate change. Actually, you'd be surprised at the number of changes that are initiated by employees. Have you ever heard of Erin Brockovich?

Your boss may not share all of this information with you because he or she may think it is more than you need to know. I think you can handle it and that you want to know, so you understand how to offer amazing ideas that contribute to the health and success of the business. If you don't understand how the business makes money, how can you perform with purpose?

I worked with a client whose employees were not billing all of their time. They worked in healthcare and often the family called the nurses to talk about their child's care or ask the nurse to stop back by for a quick visit. The nurses considered the patients their critical relationships and their job was to care for their families and help them. The company needed the nurses to bill for their time or they couldn't afford to pay the nurses. The company had built their budget on the nurse's billing 32 hours per week. The nurses were not exposed to the budget or how the company was run; they only knew the company expected 32 billable hours a week. The nurses resented this requirement because they felt it was asking them not to give quality care. What's the opportunity here?

How might we ask the nurses to help think of the best way to bill hours and provide quality care? We worked with the nurses to walk them through how the business made money. If you don't understand this in your organization, ask. Explain that you want to evaluate your critical relationships and you want to contribute to the overall success of your company. If your company isn't willing to share this information with you, stop and evaluate if you will ever be able to be successful in the culture. It's hard to make good decisions when you don't have good data, or an understanding of how things work.

Once the nurses understood the business model and could identify all of their critical relationships, not just the patients, they were able to offer suggestions on how they could improve their billing, while serving their patients. Billing went up and quality care remained the same.

You are crucial to helping your company maximize their critical relationships. Please remember, this is not a one-and-done activity. You should perform this review periodically. Things change, technology evolves, prices fluctuate. Reaching out to your relationships and analyzing the touchpoints will make your relationships stronger and be mutually beneficial.

Chapter 4 Positive Impact Points Summary

Having positive, productive, mutually beneficial relationships creates strong foundations in your business and in your personal life. Understanding what is important about those relationships and how you can make them stronger and more effective will lead to mutual success. Let's take a moment to review all you've done.

In this chapter, you:

- Defined the importance of your critical relationships
- Considered how you treat others and how you want to be treated
- Explored your impact on your relationships
- Identified areas to make relationships even better
- Considered the impact on others as you perform your duties
- Learned you should to treat your vendors like customers
- Learned relationships are yours to manage

If you haven't completed these activities yet, I recommend that you take the time to finish them before moving to chapter 5. Feel free to send any questions you have to contact@earnmethodbook.com.

"In Business it's about people. It's about relationships.   ~Kathy Ireland

CHAPTER 5
Create Your Target

In this chapter, the Positive Impact Points we will review include:

- Setting SMARTER goals
  - Goals need to be *specific, measurable,* a*greed upon, realistic, time bound,* something you are *excited* about, and *reinforceable*
- Including personal goals
  - You are always one person – focus on your whole self
- Creating a notebook or system to track your goals and have a visual representation of your progress
  - Remember the old saying, "What gets watched, gets measured"
- Sharing your ideas and enlisting help
  - Having an accountability partner increases your chances of meeting your goal
- Taking initiative
  - Raise your hand – people need the information you have to offer

- Seek out other's ideas and opinions
  - Be curious, ask a lot of questions, and you'll get a lot of great answers!

The only worksheet you'll need for this chapter is the Goal Worksheet.

You can find worksheets here: www.earnmethodbook.com.

Now let's get started with setting some goals.

What do you want for yourself? For your life? What's really important to you? Your goals need to include what you need to be happy (whatever happy looks like for you)! Where do you want to be with your career next month, next year, or in five years? Where do you want to be with volunteering? Creativity? Physical Activity? Faith? You've looked at the who, what, and how of your job, now let's look at the *YOU* in your job and create the path that's right for you. A life without goals isn't living; its surviving. I call it sleepwalking or unconscious living. If you don't set a course, how will you measure your progress? How will you know you're moving in the right direction? How will you know when you have arrived? I said earlier, "Life's a journey, not a destination," and although I believe that is true, if you never set a destination, you might end up wandering. No matter if it's a pleasant experience or not, wandering won't provide opportunities in every aspect of your life. So, setting some goals is important. You can also set goals around enjoying the journey.

If you're resistant to this or you feel yourself saying that you prefer to "let go and let God," I invite you to suspend your resistance for this chapter. I recently worked with a client, Hazel, who had this exact philosophy and found that specific goals were extremely useful to her. Hazel told me a story about choosing one word[4] to focus on for the year. She said she chose the word, *expansion* and she gained 10 pounds that year. After that experience, she became a true believer around setting very specific goals with her one word, and listening carefully to make sure it was the right word for her.

Hopefully this isn't new for you, you don't feel resistant, and you are part of your goal-setting process at work. If you aren't now, I want you to consider it part of your job. It's how you know how you are performing. I also want to make sure you set some personal goals and include what's important to you. The best-case scenario is to find meaningful work that allows you to blend your personal and work goals. If you have a personal goal to spend one Saturday every month helping those less fortunate than you, and your company partners with Habitat for Humanity, that's a win/win for you (assuming you have a safe place to live). In the same regard, if your company asks you to work overtime on Saturdays or every Sunday, that might keep you from achieving your personal goal.

I've spent a lot of time encouraging you to find an organization that matches your value set and that's important for your organization too. I've seen small business owners that encourage their employees to be involved in the community with opportunities and paid time to do so, and the employees have complained about having to do it. It did not match their personal goals. Remember, this is your life and setting goals allows you to create a path to get to where you want to be, and to create the life you want to live. If you try to create your life outside of your job, you won't have much time for living. Performing with purpose allows you to create goals to stay on your chosen path, both personally and professionally. If you're thinking you won't be able to find companies that align with what you want, I invite you to broaden your mind. Employers change their working conditions all the time to meet the needs of the talent they need to run their organization. Lots of businesses allow employees to bring their pets to work, to telecommute, and to have flexible schedules because they are adjusting to the needs of their employees. Once you have the skills to show your value, your opportunities for personal fulfillment at work will grow.

It's helpful to keep a notebook of your progress. I use the term *notebook* because it is universal, but this could be a sketchbook, a OneNote book, Google Drive folders, a white board, a cork board, a three-ring binder – whatever works for you. You need to keep track of your progress in a format that allows you to see it, like a scoreboard in sports. Imagine you are at a football game and the scoreboard goes totally blank. The game continues, but there is no visual scoreboard to tell you play-by-play exactly what's happening on the field. What do you think would happen to the crowd's involvement? The crowd needs the scoreboard to be able to track where each team is and to get excited. I have always kept track of my own performance both at home and at work, and coincidentally, I have never had a bad performance review. Well, I take it back. One time I did have a bad performance review and I'll share how this system helped me a little later in this chapter. Anytime anyone wants to talk about my performance, I open my three-ring binder with tabs representing each of my goals and ask what goal they want to discuss. Now, don't get me wrong, this isn't an organized binder; it is a mess with post-its, drawings, collage pages, photos, typed sheets, and so on. But, it does have all of the information I need to talk about *my* goals. Even if my boss assigned me goals, I still add my own, and I always include my personal goals. As I meet each goal, I put all supporting documents behind that tab and then I celebrate. You can do this electronically today but for me, it's more fun to have a tangible visual image. That doesn't make it the best way, or even the preferred way, it is just the way that works for me. Figure out what works for you, and make sure it is easy and fun for you to maintain. Your system can house as little information as you feel necessary, or as much as you want to store, as long as it tracks your progress. I'll give you a hint on this one – it takes far less time to organize information documenting your performance than it does to complain to others that your boss doesn't appreciate everything you do, or that you never seem to accomplish what you want to do in life.

Goals can be long or short term. If you've ever worked on a project, worked by yourself, or worked with a team in school, you were exposed to setting goals. Ideally, your organization does regular planning, and both your and their goals align with the overall strategy of the business. If your organization doesn't plan, and many organizations don't, then you can work with your manager to determine which goals are most meaningful and necessary to you. If your manager isn't interested in setting goals with you, then you may want to evaluate if you are in the right department or working for the right organization. How can anyone evaluate your performance without goals?

To plan your goals, use the information we've covered so far:

- Critical functions that need procedures or backups
- Critical relationships
- Job performance opportunities

Let's review some business goals you can set, like documenting how something is done, which can serve the business in many ways. Whether it is a written procedure, checklist, or YouTube video, think about how it helps in the way of training, or cross training new team members (or even getting everyone on the same page on the best way to do something). While I don't expect you to set your organization's goals, you have already done a lot with what you have discovered in the analysis you performed in the previous chapters. Take a look at the goals you have identified and in the next activity, you will write down a few to begin the goal setting process. Consider how you'd describe what you do and how you make people feel. Also, consider some personal goals or things you want to accomplish as well. Maybe you want to write a book, walk on the Appalachian trail, travel, volunteer, start a program, go back to school, read more, and so on.

Review the two goals for our grocery store cashier shown in the example Goal Worksheet below. Take note of how she includes her personal goals, which also benefit the company.

Goal Worksheet							
SMARTER = **S**pecific, **M**easurable, **A**greed Upon, **R**ealistic, **T**ime bound, **E**xcitement, **R**einforceable							
Goal Description	Benefits	Owner	Priority	Start	End	Reinforcement Schedule	Community/ Planet Impact
Smile at every customer who comes through my line	*Makes me feel better, makes customer feel better, great customer service*						
Tell 10 appropriate jokes throughout the day and record the ones that get a good reaction	*Help me build a collection of jokes that I can use in my Improv training, make customers laugh, great customer service*						

Now it's your turn! For this activity, pull up the **Goal Worksheet** you downloaded at the beginning of this chapter.

We're going to start with the first two columns and then complete the rest of the worksheet throughout this chapter. What goals do you want to accomplish? This is sometimes the hardest part. If you are having a hard time, I suggest using a blank piece of paper or your journal to do a five-minute writing exercise. To do this, ensure you are in a place where you'll be uninterrupted, and set a timer on your cell phone, computer, or watch for five minutes. Begin by writing, "The goals I want to accomplish this year are…" and continue writing for five minutes. During the five minutes, your pen or pencil cannot leave the paper; just keep writing. Let your mind wander and write whatever comes to you, even if it is your grocery list. You're not sharing this list with anyone, so feel free to shred it when you are done. When you are finished, move to Step 1 to complete the activity.

STEP 1: In the **Goal Description** column, start entering your goals. Be sure the description of the goal is specific and easily understood by others because you are going to share these goals with your friends, colleagues, and manager. Think of as many goals as you can. You can always narrow down the list later if you have too many, but for right now, make that list as long as possible.

STEP 2: Next, in the **Benefits** column, document the advantages of your goals. Who is going to benefit from those goals? How are they going to benefit? What will you attain from setting the goal? How will your work, company, or life be better when you attain this goal? Knowing the benefit or the *why* of your goal will help you get excited about your goal and celebrate your success.

How many goals did you come up with? You can complete this list after you read this chapter, but I do want you to have a few goals documented to make sure the goal is written in the best way to help you achieve it. I like to think of goals as opportunities. You may have been exposed to SMART goals,[1] but I have added two letters for you to make your goals SMARTER: E for *Excitement* and R for *Reinforcement*.

Consider the goals you just wrote and give them the SMARTER test by reading the goal and asking these questions: Do you feel excitement around the goal? Is the goal fun? Can you make it fun? Can you celebrate along the way or add some sort of game? Will it be reinforced? What happens if you don't do it?

Using the cashier example goal, "Smile at every customer who comes through my line," is this goal *specific*? Yes, our cashier knows to smile at every customer who comes through her line. Is it *measurable*? Yes. One way she can measure this is to have a mirror and a piece of paper. As each new customer enters her line, she could look at her face in the mirror, ensure she is smiling and give herself a checkmark. Is it *agreed upon*? We'll assume that she agreed upon this goal with her manager. Is it *realistic*? It is a realistic goal for her because she normally smiles at everyone, and the *time bound* for this goal is every day, every customer. Is she *excited* about it? Our cashier is excited about this because she wants to be a comedian one day, and part of her act is being super friendly. So, smiling at every customer allows her to work on this goal. Is it *reinforceable*? It is and her manager gives her the thumbs up and positive feedback for smiling every time she works.

Use the following chart and ask yourself each question to make sure all of the elements are included in your goals.

---

[1] The SMART acronym first appeared in the November 1981 issue of *Management Review* written by George Doran, Arthur Miller, and James Cunningham.

S	*Is it specific?* Making something better is a nice idea, but it's not specific. Improving production by 10% or making three more sales calls per week – those are specific.
M	*Is it measurable?* If you can't measure it, how will you know when it is completed?
A	*Is it agreed upon?* Get buy in from those who are affected by what you are trying to accomplish.
R	*Is it realistic?* Challenge your assumptions! You may need to break a big goal into more manageable pieces.
T	*Is it time bound?* Have a time table, set due date milestones, and stick to them.
E	*Are you excited about it?* Create excitement around achieving the goal, schedule a celebration, and celebrate successes along the way.
R	*Is it reinforceable?* Determine the reinforcement needed to accomplish the goal. What's in it for you? For others?

Take some time now to look at the goals you wrote earlier and make sure they are SMARTER. Add to or change them as you ask the questions to ensure each of your goals is SMARTER.

Excellent. Now you have SMARTER goals you can work with that will benefit both you and your organization. Using these goals will help you perform with purpose. In order to maximize your performance, you'll need to know a few more things about these goals, like their priority, when they need to be completed, the reinforcement schedule (used from the *R* in SMARTER), and if they have a community/planet impact. Why do you care if they have an impact on your community or planet? One reason you might care is because we all play a part in the wellbeing of our communities and planet, and business has the potential to have the greatest positive impact. If you don't know what the impact is right now, that is fine. Just leave it blank and give it some thought.

Now, complete the **Goal Worksheet** you began earlier.

STEP 3: In the **Owner** column, document who owns this goal. In most cases, it will be you. But in other cases, it may be your manager or someone who assigned you the goal.

STEP 4: In the **Priority** column, rank your goals. This is a very important. Although all of your goals are important, they are not going to have the same priority. Some goals will need to be done before others, so it is important to rank the goals in order of priority. I suggest you use the following system to rank them:

A: Very important goal - I need to focus my attention to get this goal done.

B: Important goal - I need to focus on this goal and look forward to starting it or working on it after I complete my A goals.

C: Future goal - either it has a delayed start time or I need to complete another goal to start this goal.

D: Low priority goal - this is not important and something I'll work on if I have extra time.

Now, cross off all of the **D** goals. If a goal is not important to you, it should not be on this list.

STEP 5: In the **Start** column, enter the date you are going to start your goal. Once you choose this date, commit to it.

The Association for Talent Development (ATD) did a study on accountability and found that you have a 65% chance of completing a goal if you commit to someone. And if you have a specific accountability appointment with a person you commit to, you increase your chance of success by up to 95%. So, find an accountability partner and share the start date of your goal.

Step 6: In the **End** column, estimate and enter the date your goal will be complete. Also share this date with your accountability partner.

Step 7: In the **Reinforcement Schedule** column, determine and enter how your progress on your goal will be reinforced. This step will help you stay on track.

In our grocery store example, the cashier was reinforced by both the feeling of accomplishment creating her tick mark sheet with the mirror, and by her manager giving her positive feedback for her behavior. Your reinforcement schedule often keeps you going. Think of it in terms of training an animal. If you want a dog to sit, you would give the dog a specific command – Sit. You might also give the dog some hand signals or help, and as soon as the dog sits, he is rewarded with a treat or praise. You would continue giving the dog a treat or praise until the sit command was automatic, and then you'd phase out treats for that command and add another command. That's essentially what you are trying to do for yourself. Create a reinforcement that is a reward for accomplishing a step in your goal. Your reinforcement can be having a report that shows you met your goal, showing your manager how you met your goal, or a scorecard that you write on each day showing your progress. It just needs to be positive and motivate you so you can celebrate how well you are doing. I recommend you celebrate every single day how great you are doing. Think about how often you celebrate a dog in training – every single time the dog performs the command, there is a celebration. Celebrate often! Do a dance, give yourself an air high five, smile, and say "Yes!" Make a sign that says 100% and put it on your computer, do a victory lap around the office, text a friend, and celebrate every milestone along the way to meeting your goal.

Step 8: In the **Community/Planet Impact** column, enter goals you want to achieve to contribute to your community or a healthy planet. This may be new to you, but I feel it is important. Spend some time thinking about how your goal impacts your community and the planet. The results of your accomplished goals will leave a lasting, positive impact on your business, and create both satisfaction and opportunities for you.

I had an employee one time who used to set these types of goals. We met every few weeks to review her goals and to talk about her performance, and every so often she would add a new goal to her list that I'd never even considered. We started showing episodes of The Office during lunch, adding afternoon celebrations to new-hire training, created a Spirit Week, and developed a SharePoint Learning Lab. She was a very valuable employee and she knew it. She also shared her personal goals, which we were able to integrate into her work. Work became fun for her and she continued to set more and more goals, expanding her capacity, and growing both personally and professionally. It's easier to do with a good manager, but it's possible to do with any manager.

When you're finished completing the Goal Worksheet, schedule a meeting with your manager to discuss.

Now, about that bad performance review I eluded to earlier. Early in my career, in about my fifth job (I've had about 15), my boss scheduled my performance review. He didn't ask me for any input in advance, but I had my three-ring binder, so I brought it along. As I sat through the performance review, he rated me consistently a three out of five in every category. He would read each question, his rating, and his comments on every single page, without looking up or asking me for any feedback. When he was finished, he said, "Do you have any questions?" I was young and up to this point in my career, I had received raving reviews from my supervisors, so I didn't understand the low rating. Three out of five isn't actually a low rating at all; it means I am doing what is expected in my job. Since I had always received fives before, it felt low. I couldn't think of any questions, so I said no and walked away with my review and my binder, which I never even bothered to open during the conversation.

Later that evening, I thought about the conversation and the review, and looked through my binder. I realized that a lot of the work I had done had not been discussed and I wanted to have another conversation. I emailed my supervisor and asked for a follow-up conversation. He replied saying he was too busy to talk with me, that I had the opportunity to ask my questions in the meeting with him, and since I didn't, he wouldn't be able to accommodate me now.

I did not think this was fair and just as Patterson, Grenny, McMillan, and Switzler say in Crucial Conversations,[5] "If you don't talk it out, you'll act it out." I did just that with my attitude and performance. My supervisor may have been too busy to talk with me, but his manager noticed the shift in my behavior and requested a meeting with me. In the meeting, she asked why I seemed unhappy. I retrieved my three-ring binder and went over my performance review with her and the accomplishments I had listed under each tab. She was so impressed that she decided to promote me, and my previous supervisor became my peer. When you set goals, expand your capabilities and keep track of your progress. You're not average!

Chapter 5 Points of Impact Summary

We've done a lot in this chapter. Let's take a moment now and recap all you've done.

In this chapter, you:

- Set SMARTER goals for yourself
- Included personal goals
- Created a notebook or system to track your goals
- Shared your ideas and enlisted help
- Took initiative
- Sought out other people's ideas and opinions

"If you don't know where you are going, any road will get you there."

~Lewis Carroll

CHAPTER 6
What Gets Measured

In this chapter, the Positive Impact Points we will review include:

- Understanding what current measures exist for what you do
  - The four Ws of the tasks you perform: Who, What, When and WHIIDI (what happens if I do it?)
- Understanding where the information comes from and who is looking at it
  - Is there a report? Dashboard? Does it feed into something else?
- Taking responsibility for what is expected of you in the performance of your critical functions and interactions
  - Your performance is your responsibility and compensating you for it fairly is your company's responsibility
  - Be prepared to show your value
- Identifying new or more meaningful measurements if they don't currently exist
  - You are most informed about the work you do

- • Create meaningful measurements
- ▪ Knowing how your performance is measured
  - • Work with your manager on measuring your performance

The worksheets you'll need include:

- ▪ The Four Ws of Accountability
- ▪ Measurement Tracking Worksheet

You can find worksheets here: www.earnmethodbook.com.

Now let's get started by reviewing your SMARTER goals and determine the best way to measure when they are achieved. Think of it as creating the right measurements to show on a scoreboard. Not only would it not be fun to watch a game without a scoreboard, but the information on the scoreboard drives what we are watching. When you watch a football game, the scoreboard shows you not only the score and who's ahead, but how much time is left in the game, where the players are on the field, how many timeouts they have available – it gives you the information to track and measure what your preferred team is doing. This is true in all sporting events. They want to give you enough information to stay engaged. This is what we want to do with your job; measure the right information to not only show how you are succeeding, but also to keep you and your manger engaged in the work you are doing.

This information will let you know if you are improving by comparing how you are doing against the performance necessary in your role in the organization. If your manager cannot tell you specifically what you need to accomplish, then how will they rate your performance? A performance rating rates your performance against expectations. Are you comfortable having your manager's expectations for your job living in your managers head, or do you want them documented so you know exactly what they are? Statistics and data can validate performance. Identify areas that need attention, expose opportunities for change, show where you need improvement, or indicate when it's time to CELEBRATE.

When looking at measurements, you may be interested in financial statistics, customer satisfaction, success rates, rework, quantity, quality, time, costs, or performance against a standard or a group. Let's take a minute to look at the measurements and feedback you currently get, or don't get in your current job, and think about what will help you with measuring your goals. Is there a measurement that would motivate you? Do you know what success looks like? Do you have a lot of data but no way to measure it? Having pure data without any expectation or standard is interesting but not very useful in measuring your performance in your role.

Let's think about the grocery store opportunity we identified of adding the monitors in the checkout line. What type of measurements could we use to determine if it is successful in the store? We could rate customer satisfaction, impulse buys, or customer loyalty. Since we set our SMARTER goals, we know what we want them to be, and we can compare if we are on track. Now you give it a try.

For this activity, pull up **The Four Ws of Accountability** worksheet you downloaded at the beginning of this chapter. You are going to use the four W questions to make sure you have all the information you need to create solid measurements.

The Four Ws of Accountability

When looking at the tasks you perform daily, weekly, or monthly in your job, ask the following four W questions:

Task Name:_____

- **Who** is working on the task? Will my performance be rated for my input or for the team's performance?
- **What** specifically is being measured in the task I perform? The outcome? Interim steps? Know what is being measured and what you are accountable for.
- **When** do the measurements occur? If your job is part of an assembly line, do they measure your work as part of a final product or immediately after it's done? If it is at the end, does anything else affect the work that you did?

> • **WHIIDI** (what happens if I do it?) What happens if you do perform your task correctly? How do the results reflect in your performance review, promotion, pay, bonus? Meeting expectations of your manager? Contributing to your team's results?

STEP 1: On the **Task Name** line, enter the name of the task you want to work on first.

STEP 2: Start with **Who** and answer the questions to define who does what to accomplish the goal.

Using the monitors in the grocery line example, the "who" in the measurement would be whoever's task it was to create the programming shown on the TV monitors. The programming would be measured to determine if it holds the child's attention long enough for the parent/guardian to look at the impulse buys for 1-2 minutes. The "who" in this measurement would not be the cashier because the cashier is not performing a measurable task. If the cashier was measured on how many impulse buys were sold in her lane, then the cashier would need to determine what measurable actions she could take to accomplish this goal, and discuss those actions with her manager.

STEP 3: Next, review the **What** questions and define what specifically is being measured with the task you perform.

In our cashier SMARTER goal example, we know the cashier is responsible to smile at 100% of the customers who come through her lane. She knows this is a self-measurement she is keeping herself with tally marks. Additionally, she may learn that her manager is auditing her for accuracy by randomly watching her interact with five customers a day.

STEP 4: For the **When** questions, determine when the measurements occur. This is important because if the measurement occurs after the work has been completed, it's possible that something else is included in the measurement besides just the work you are doing.

In our cashier example, the cashier may be rated on balancing the money in her register, so that she doesn't make any mistakes counting or giving back change to a customer. If the drawer is reconciled at the end of the night and more than one cashier uses the same drawer, that measurement wouldn't only be for the one cashier's performance, and the cashier wouldn't have any control of the results.

STEP 4: Lastly, assess and define what happens when you perform your tasks correctly. This is important because it lets you know the real accountability for the task you are performing. Do you get recognized? Does it make your job easier? Going back to the EARN Method, determine if there are reinforcements for ending the task. If there is no accountability for you if you don't do the task, but you determine it is a task you need to nurture, then create self-accountability and a measurement around it. If you feel like you're doing a lot of work and it is not being appreciated, self-accountability will help you!

In our cashier example, one of her goals is to clean her belt with cleanser every hour. This ensures her belt is dry and germ free. If no one ever checks and her manager doesn't care or rate her on it, this may not seem like an important goal. If the cashier knows this is the best way to offer the customer a clean, germ-free environment, and helps ensure the food stays clean, she might set some self-accountability. She can do this by giving herself a check box to keep track of cleaning her belt every hour, and then sharing with her manager how she keeps track of the goal.

Managers make mistakes and forget things, so going through this process with your goals and measurements will make sure you are doing the right things, the right way at the right time. Managers can only be as good as their employees because your manager's main job is to make sure you do yours.

Now that you have this information, what do you do with it? Is it visible to other areas or customers, used for coaching and evaluation, rewards or penalties? How do you know where you are? What is the benefit derived from the information? Still working with our cashier and using the monitor example, how do you think it will help you as a cashier to know what's being measured? If you know the objectives from the program development team, you might make a comment about the video, or you might make sure the monitors are working correctly, turned on, and so on. You might straighten your impulse buy baskets to make sure they are accessible. Think of how you respond when you know what the measurement is, and what specifically is expected of you.

I also want to review a few other categories for your measurements. You've looked at what is being measured, now let's determine what the recipient does with the information. If the recipient can't find a benefit, or even worse doesn't need it, is it useful? Let me give you an example.

I worked for a bank as collection manager in a previous life and was charged with improving their collection performance. The first month on the job I spent reviewing the various procedures and activities of the units. I noticed activity reduced significantly the last two to three days of the month. When I asked why, I was told the staff was busy preparing a report that was due the first day of the month to the CFO, who was new to his job too. In fact, he had only been on the job for about six months himself. I let the team continue to work on the report and told them I wanted to personally deliver the information to the CFO as soon as they were done. After hours of labor, detailing collections on each account, the report was ready. I walked into the CFO's office with the report and said, "Here is the monthly collection report. Can I ask what you do with it?" He looked me straight in the eye and said, "You know, I haven't really had a chance to focus on that." Sound familiar? He pointed to his credenza behind him where there was a stack of reports and said, "I have just been stacking them up here." I explained that the compilation of this data basically took the department to its knees at a time each month when labor should be focused on collecting, not reporting. I then asked what information he really needed, so we could refocus employees on what was truly important. It turns out, the former CFO didn't use the report either; it was a leftover from a previous manager in the collection area who thought it was a good idea. I have seen this type of situation over and over in my career. Things are done because they have always been done. That's why it is important to be conscious - to ask "why" and what the benefit is to the recipient. If they can't tell you or you don't know, it will benefit everyone to find out. Over the years, I've asked a lot of stupid questions and when I started getting stupid answers, I knew I was on to something.

You also need to consider the source of data. This is important because if you are getting your measurement data from another system, you want to make sure that system is set up to send you the data with the frequency you need it. For instance, if you are being measured by the average number of calls you take per day, you want to see the number of calls you take daily. That way, if you need to make any adjustments, you can make them that day. A monthly report detailing each day won't be as effective because you may forget the specifics of the day. Or, if you are being measured on quality, you will want to know who is monitoring your quality and how close to real time you will receive feedback. You also want to know your deadlines. Remember, if you don't know what is being measured, you cannot effectively perform with purpose.

Earlier I discussed reinforcements using SMARTER goals. These reinforcements are essential to meeting deadlines. You don't need to wait for someone to do this for you; you already know how to self-manage. If you wait for someone else to do these things for you, then you often don't get the results you want. I want YOU to be the one who controls the results you want to see so you can get where you want to go.

I worked with a manager one time who was exasperated because his employee was not doing what he wanted him to do. He had set SMART goals with the employee and even gone as far as to state what the celebration would be for the *E* in **SMARTER**. My first question to the manager was, "What happens when the employee doesn't do it?" The manager started explaining how it causes frustration and more work for the other people on the team. I interrupted him, "What happens to the employee?" That's the same question I had you assess – what happens if you don't do it? If you have a goal and you aren't able to meet it, talk to someone about it. They will either help you change the deadline or change whatever obstacles are in your way. Managers are often taught that their role is to remove your obstacles - let them fulfill their duty. The deadline for a measurement is important! If nothing happens when you don't do it, go back to your four Ws and create your own accountability.

I want to take measurements a bit further and put your measurements into the Measurement Tracking Worksheet. I know I'm putting a lot of emphasis on this and that is because this is the most important step in the process. Your goal in any job is to produce measurable results that have value for the company and align with the company's goals, values, and, mission. Measurement tracking allows you to do this.

For this activity, pull up the **Measurement Tracking Worksheet** you downloaded at the beginning of this chapter.

Measurement Tracking Worksheet						
What is being measured?	Source	Owner	Frequency	Deadline	Recipient	Benefit to Recipient
Impulse buys	*Report by Time Frames*	*Store Manager*	*Daily*	*12:00 am – report autoruns at that time*	*Shift Supervisor*	*Tracks higher selling items for placement and restocking*
Customer Satisfaction	*Third party vendor survey*	*Store Manager*	*Prints on every receipt*	*Time of transaction*	*Customer*	*If they respond, they are eligible for a monthly drawing to win a $500 gift card for your store*

STEP 1: In the first column, document what is being measured. Use your answers to the **What** questions on your **Four Ws of Accountability** worksheet.

STEP 2: In the **Source** column, enter the source the data is collected from, for example, a report, tick sheet, system, accounting, and so on.

STEP 3: In the **Owner** column, identify the name or role of who owns the measurement, or who is going to make sure the performance is measured and monitor the results.

STEP 4: In the **Frequency** column, enter how often the performance will be measured, for example, daily, weekly, monthly, and so on.

STEP 5: In the **Deadline** column, enter the timeframe for the data to be collected, for example, at the end of every shift, weekly, monthly report, and so on.

STEP 6: In the **Recipient** column, identify who should receive this data. Who needs to know the task or performance was done correctly and on time?

STEP 7: In the **Benefit to Recipient** column, document the benefit of the recipient knowing this information.

Being able to track and measure this information will change the way you look at your work. When you understand how your work fits into the big picture and the importance of your work to someone else, it changes the way you look at it.

I remember working with a company that ordered service processing from a process server. This means they hired an outside vendor to personally deliver legal papers and notices to people, which they called "serving" the person. The company had a performance problem on their team because the employees were not putting the right information in their computer system. The process server received their information directly from the company's system, so they could not serve the right people with the right documents if the information was not entered correctly. The company continued to train their employees on how to enter the information into the computer system, and they continued to have mistakes. As a consultant, the first thing I did was ask employees to explain their process. They understood how to enter the information on to the computer screen and told me how they chose which file to check. I then asked them what the recipient (the process server) was doing with that information. They didn't know, so I told them I would find out. I later went back to the team and explained the process server's job. I explained how the information was transferred to the process server, what the process server did when they received the information, and what they sent back to the company after they had served the person (delivered the documents). Once the team knew how the recipient was using the information, their error rates dropped significantly. They were able to see the big picture.

That's the point of defining your measurements. As you put together the big picture in your company, you will start to realize how important the work is that you do every day, and the importance of sharing with others the results you achieve.

Chapter 6 Positive Impact Points Summary

Do you feel like you have done a lot of work in this chapter? You have!
In this chapter, you:

- Created measurements for the work you do
- Determined who is working on the task being measured
- Determined what needs to be measured and when
- Identified what happens if you don't do a task and created self-management for tasks with no follow-up by your manager
- Took responsibility for your performance
- Made sure you understand the value of your tasks for the recipient

---

"If you can't measure it, you can't improve it."   *~Peter Drucker*

CHAPTER 7
Your Performance

In this chapter, the Positive Impact Points we will review include:

- Continuing to take responsibility for your performance
  - You own your performance
- Looking for ways to learn and grow – asking questions
  - Think of the questions a three-year-old would ask and move from a place of curiosity
- Respecting people's time
  - Clear, concise communication is easier for everyone involved – use your tools
- Stay in the game and keep your eye on the target
  - Like in archery, your eye stays on the target, not the arrow
  - My tools perfected your form – it's time for you to hit the target!
  - A bull's eye is not the only measurement

You will not need any additional worksheets for this chapter. However, I will be referring to Ideas to Consider, which you can find here: www. earnmethodbook.com.

Now, let's take a deeper look at your performance. I firmly believe that no one gets up in the morning with the intent to perform poorly or disappoint their manager. I do acknowledge however, that many managers and management systems fail at setting expectations, measuring results, and giving timely and constructive feedback to their employees. A good indicator of this is if your manager says to you, "Why didn't you do this?" Anytime I hear that, it is a red flag to me that there are no clear expectations. The reason is because if you and your manager had reviewed your critical functions, critical relationships, set SMARTER goals, and set up measurements and accountability, your manager would say, "Our goal is XXX, can we talk about the process you followed when ..." Doing the work you've done so far will eliminate the *surprises* of your work day and it will make sure your manager supports you when talking with customers. Has your manager or business owner ever received a call from a customer and told the customer, "I don't know why they didn't do that. Very disappointing. I will make sure someone fixes that immediately." That's another red flag that you don't have clear, consistent processes. If you did, the manager/business owner would respond, "That doesn't sound like <insert your name here> or our process. I'll look into what happened." Think about your culture and your manager. What is your manager likely to say if a customer calls and complains about your work? What do you want them to say?

Your performance should not be a surprise to anyone, most of all you! Take the time to own your performance; it is the most important to you. Are all your critical functions and relationships covered? If not, add them to your worksheet. Think about all of the areas we discussed, like where the best place is to get the information. What should the standard be if one doesn't exist? Who needs this information? What opportunities exist to save time or money, or improve performance or satisfaction? Many employees may say their managers should be considering all of this, not them. But you know that you are in the driver's seat of your own performance. You also know that doing this makes you a very valuable asset to your organization, and a prize for a competitor to recruit. Getting this data right helps you be the best you can be at doing what you do. As an employee, taking an interest in your performance and always striving to make things better sets you up for more success, and ultimately leads to better economic outcomes. I guess that is why many people use sports analogies when they look at businesses; I know I do it all the time. As a comparison for great measurements, I use statistics like batting averages, yards per carry, shots on goal, or strokes to par. Of course, when you do this, you need to make sure the person you are speaking to has some sort of reference for what you are talking about. Ask if they have ever watched a baseball game or say, "You know how in basketball they..." I often challenge employees to go for the three-pointer, even if they are blindfolded and shooting from half court. Even if I have to explain the measurement first, the analogy is still powerful.

You are measured against a standard or compared to others to determine whether you're performing well; know what that standard or measurement is. This data also points to areas that may need emphasis to get your competitive juices flowing. Like I said earlier, no one wakes up and thinks, *what can I screw up at work today?* I believe everyone has an honest desire to do well and that's why you've been documenting what *doing well* looks like.

When you end each day, you should know what you accomplished and where it falls on your scale from *EHH* to *WOW!*

An important outcome is to celebrate your achievements and improvements, as well as seeking coaching to improve results. A measurement ignored is a measurement wasted, so be sure you are tracking results and seek to maximize your performance. Using the EARN Method will help you seek what opportunities are available for you by allowing you to spend your time on the right things. If you work for a company that started with three people doing the work and moved into an assembly line process, the EARN Method will help you identify how to create efficiencies. Likewise, if you work for a company that has ever been through a merger or acquisition, the EARN Method may keep you busy for months or years. It is so important to identify what is important today. Marshall Goldsmith wrote a great book, *What Got You Here Won't Get You There* for leaders that emphasizes the need to change your style and strategy as you move to different levels in your career. The same is true for companies and for you. You need to continue to evaluate, adapt, and adopt to your current landscape. Doing what has always been done causes frustration, needless work, additional steps, and inefficiencies.

The work you've done allows you to be aware of trends and act on what you see. Ignoring the results that you get, especially if it is bad, helps to either reinforce the behavior you're getting or stop someone from doing it again.

I hear people focus on generational terms like Baby Boomers, Gen Xers and Millennials all the time. I ask that you to put all of that aside. This system works for you no matter what generation you identify with, and where you are in your career. We're looking at performance. We're looking at who you are, what's important to you, what your job is, how that aligns with your personal goals, how to have standards of performance, how to set SMARTER goals, and how to track and measure those goals. Your age, background, and beliefs are only relevant as to what is important to you. My best boss ever often said, "The one with the most data wins," and I am asking you to focus on data. Measurements are measurements and if you define what good customer service is, you can measure how well you are delivering it, regardless of external factors. If you don't know what the measurement is, how can you expect to meet the standard? You will also know when to change the standard. When you are doing the same thing and getting different results, it's time to take a look at what you're doing.

If you spent your money to hire someone to do something for you, let's say wash your car, what would you compare their work against? Is it how you would wash your car? If it is, you may be disappointed. I may not wash a car with as much diligence and care as you do. How would you tell me what you want? Would you say, "Just wash it like I wash it"? If you said that, would you expect me to have questions? You need to treat your job in that same way and ask those same questions.

When I coach managers, they often say things like, "My employees just don't get it!" And when they say that, I ask them, "Do you believe your employees get up every day and come to work with the intention of not performing well?" Your manager can not read your mind, and they do not know if something is unclear to you. You need to ask them questions and have them clarify what they want. To help you with that, I want to let you in on a little secret – your boss doesn't know that much more than you do. Seriously. They know things from experience, but besides experience and training, they are just the same as you are. It's kind of like the difference between children and adults. Children often think adults have all the answers, until they become adults and then they figure out we're just winging it. We do have more experience, but that doesn't mean we have all the answers, and if you don't believe me, spend the day with a three-year-old and observe the questions they ask you. I guarantee you at some point you will respond, "I don't know." You may respond in frustration, but if you are really curious, you'll soon realize that you can't answer a lot of the three-year-old's questions, like why the power grid was laid out in your town that way, why animals respond the way they do, or where the concrete came from that laid the foundation for your house. Your manager may not be able to answer your questions either, and they may get frustrated or dismiss you when you ask. However, if you use the forms we've reviewed and give your input and specific examples, you will be able to clarify what your job expectations are.

When I was young, I had this belief that high school issues happened in high school, but when you grew up and went into the "real" world, people would communicate better, bullying would stop, you'd find a job that played to your strengths, and there would be no drama. That "real" world isn't real, and your managers expectations of your performance may not be real either if you aren't using tools and measurements to evaluate them. If you have a functioning crystal ball that allows you to read your manager's mind, use that. If you don't, use the tools we've reviewed to create performance standards you can meet.

Why do you want to take this on as your responsibility? Because this is *your life.* I've had the opportunity to sit with a few friends at the end of their lives and I know for them, this mattered. It mattered that they had personal goals, that they aligned their goals with their work, and that they had accomplishments. What you do *matters!*

I actually started this work with a previous boss of mine who passed away very young. She's the one who taught me to include my personal goals in my plan, or I would never meet them. She told me that if I waited for a time when I was ready to start accomplishing my goals, I may never aim to achieve them because we aren't ever really ready. We need to look at possibilities and dream of what we'd do if we were brave and had no obstacles or barriers. If your current organization won't allow you to do this, SMARTLY, start looking for an organization that will. Don't leave your job without another job if you can't afford to, but don't stay in a job that doesn't meet your personal needs and expect to somehow miraculously become happy. There are a lot of organizations out there who want employees with values and value their employees. Find those employers and work to create a better you, a better life, and a better community.

I talk with a colleague of mine frequently and a common phrase for us is, "Are you expecting them to be like you?" It's so common for us to have standards in our mind that are the way we would do things and to measure others against it. Writing it all down and discussing it assures everyone is speaking the same language about the same big picture.

I started putting together a list of things I thought might help you establish good business practices. Based on the ideas and feedback I receive from my readers, I will be adding to this list on www.earnmethodbook.com. So, please let me know your suggestions.

Ideas to Consider

- Update your voice mail and email when you are away from the office.
- Offer your assistance to others when you have a time. Teamwork gives you the benefit of being productive and learning something new.
- Respect closed doors.
- Use the company's resources as carefully as you would your own. For example, when processing bills, invoices, and so on, question it if it seems out of line.
- Return phone calls and emails promptly.
- Learn to identify and avoid time wasters. For example, if someone takes too much of your time on non-business-related conversation, find a polite way to conclude the discussion.
- Be on time – your schedule affects others. Backlogs can be avoided when you are available and prompt.
- Take the time to hire good people.
- Get it right the first time and double check your work.
- Don't overreact or lose your cool – be the stabilizing force.

- When managing others, provide continual constructive feedback to your staff, refuse to accept mediocrity, and deal with people problems without delay.
- Meetings should begin on time, stay on track, and adjourn promptly. Be sure to assign ownership to each task to ensure you know who is responsible to do what by when.
- Encourage your staff to suggest solutions when they bring you problems.
- Allow people to make mistakes (we are all human); make it a learning opportunity. If you make a mistake, learn from it, and don't make the same one over and over (tolerance has its limits).
- Keep good records in case someone else needs to know what has transpired. History is easier to record than to reconstruct.
- Be open-minded and willing to consider other's suggestions; know your own bias and compensate whenever appropriate.
- Fix the root cause – don't just treat the symptoms.
- Listen. Truly listening is a vital skill and means not interrupting or thinking of other things while someone is talking, or what your response is going to be until it is your time to respond.
- Learn to delegate effectively, but make sure to select the right employee and the assignment is well understood.
- Whenever possible, handle your problems yourself – don't "pass the buck."
- Cross-train to provide for back-up on critical tasks.
- Understand the job you are doing to avoid mistakes and recognize exceptions that require special handling.
- Brainstorm with fellow employees on difficult and/or important decisions.
- Practice good communication.
- Organize tasks to logically fit together in order to optimize efficiency.
- Use economic reasoning; sometimes you must do what makes sense financially, versus what the procedure says, or what is in your job description.
- Develop a "suspense" system to ensure adequate follow-up.
- Be flexible and cooperative to become more productive.

- Be nice, say please and thank you.
- List and prioritize goals – short and long term. Prepare a daily "to-do" list to help plan daily activities and use a calendar to plan ahead.
- Tell the truth and seek the truth. Get all the data and confirm it, if necessary before you make a decision.
- Block out the negatives (e.g., can't, won't work) and surround yourself with a good group of mentors and trusted coworkers to bounce off your crazy ideas.
- Touch work once – focus, decide, and execute.
- Trust people; without trust, it makes it tough to delegate anything. Most people will rise to the occasion because they don't want to disappoint you (mutual respect and trust).
- Success breeds happiness (if you are doing things that are important to *you*). Winning feels good and makes you want to do whatever you did again.
- Don't take yourself too seriously.
- Take time to laugh and make other people laugh.
- Have some fun!

This list is long and I look forward to it continuing to grow. Every idea won't be a good one for you because we all have individual preferences and things to consider. Only practice the ones that resonate with you and be true to yourself. You are the best person to do whatever you choose to do in this world – do it as only you can!

You are responsible to create the work life you want, and your actions will dictate how others treat you. I've assumed that your manager or management does not have a crystal ball. But if they do, can you please tell me how they obtained it? Sometimes the hardest part of this whole process is figuring out how to say what you want to say.

I want to give you my final story as your commencement speech. I have never been asked to deliver a commencement speech, but I feel like you've just graduated from my program, and I know if I were giving a commencement speech, it would be like this. Now that I think about it, I wonder why no one has ever asked me to deliver their commencement speech? If you hear someone talking about it, can you recommend me? I'm adding that to my bucket list as a personal goal.

So, you want to be a change agent? It is not easy. Conversations about improvement will depend on the openness of your culture, whether it embraces innovation, whole-system communication, and so on. Sometimes politics also plays a part. I have always subscribed to what I call the Vidal Sassoon strategy – "Sassooning." Years ago, they had a tag line in their commercials, "If you don't look good, we don't look good![6]" I have always used that approach when working with my superiors. I approached things from their perspective, keeping in mind what I was proposing made their lives easier, and letting them take credit if they wanted. After all, they were just people like me who wanted to be recognized for doing good work. Good leaders take responsibility for the challenges, don't lay blame, and share the credit in successes. But as we know, not all leaders are good, and you will find out quickly about the character of your manager if you "Sassoon." If your goal is to make things better, who gets credit shouldn't matter. Your work speaks for itself. If your boss is a complete horse's rear end, you can make the best of it as you look for a better opportunity somewhere else – and I do encourage you to start that search sooner as opposed to later. There is no use waiting until you are bitter to find a new opportunity. They are out there. Managers are employees too, so keep in mind that everybody has a boss, and everyone has their own personal issues. Show up reframing the problems as opportunities. Likely, whatever you are addressing isn't something new. It may be something management is conscious of, but they don't feel like they have the time to get to it, or simply don't have a good solution yet.

Here are some import things to consider when "Sassooning:"

• **Be Respectful**

Ask questions, get clarification, and set goals. Remember, if you are challenging the status quo, you need to challenge respectfully. When you are told you can't do something, ask for specifics as to why not. Likewise, have specifics for your position, feelings, and instincts. Common sense is only common to you. Plan for the worst and hope for the best, but hope is never a strategy. Be sure to focus on the smallest things you can do that will have the biggest impact. Have comparisons to the current reality and the possibilities. Terms like *satisfaction* or *excellence* always have a spectrum. Determine what the current reality is and how your solution supports it. Look to the future. What happens if you don't do anything, and what are the possible outcomes of your proposal?

• **Listen and Seek Consensus**

There is more than one way to do anything. Strive to find the best way to accomplish what you are proposing to change and strive for consensus. Too many times, we don't seek compromise, consider politics, or really understand what we're willing to accept. What can others live with and support?

• **Be a Lifelong Learner**

We all have the capacity to learn and evolve in the world – every single one of us. We continually learn better technology, medicine, modern conveniences, and so on. We are creatures of habit, but we are also curious. Unfortunately, we lose some of that curiosity as we get older by creating bad habits. We should adopt a childlike wonder as we look to approach change and ask a lot of questions. Be open to new ideas and seek out other ideas and opinions. Don't be afraid to not know – sometimes this is where the best learning happens.

- **Be innovative**

Find ways to create or add value to the business or unit you work in. Anything we are doing can be done better over time. We need to be observers and students and look for opportunities for transformation. You must have passion and enthusiasm and then channel your passion and abilities to improve and create value where you are, and in the world around you. When you approach others with your ideas, outline the virtues, what success can be gained, and what pain can be avoided.

- **Be responsible**

Take responsibility for your actions. Too often we are looking to lay blame for our outcomes. I submit we must first look inward to address our contribution to the results we are getting. It is too convenient (and quite frankly, lazy) to look to place blame when things don't go our way. Anything worth doing, is worth doing well. You must commit to do the things necessary to achieve whatever goals you set, and strive to overcome the obstacles and curve balls that life presents you. No one can (or should) do it for you. At the end of the day, you are ultimately responsible for where you end up!

- **Believe in yourself**

Know your strengths and believe in yourself. Do what you are good at and find others who excel where you don't. No one is good at everything. What you do matters. Give yourself credit where credit is due and stop waiting for others to recognize your brilliance. You should be the first person to celebrate you and to talk about what you do well. If you practice, you will be able to do this with confidence and it will not be bragging or tooting your own horn, though I do believe in doing this respectfully. I'm not sure why we don't celebrate our achievements more and spend time talking about what we accomplished, but we should. If you want people to realize how great you are, make sure that is the story you are telling.

- **Be Brave**

It is not easy to stand up and take the bull by the horns proclaiming you are captain of your own ship. Brené Brown[7] talks about being both vulnerable and brave, and you will need to be both. Remember that your supervisor, manager, director, or CFO doesn't know that much more than you do. They do have experience and training, but that doesn't mean they have all the answers. Your input is valuable too and you need to be brave enough to learn to respectfully communicate your ideas, your values, and your strengths. I believe you can do this and we haven't even met. I know you will use data, goals, and defined measurements to speak your truth. I remember years ago my mother was dying and I would visit her daily at the hospital. Occasionally, I would have to leave her bedside so the nurses could attend to her. I would go to a small waiting room in the oncology unit to wait to be called back. On the wall in the waiting room was as simple message someone had crocheted and hung in a frame, "Change, of any sort, requires courage." That sentence has resonated with me ever since. The pain of loss, the idea of failure, the uncertainty of a new situation; all create varying levels of anxiety. Summoning the strength and courage to stand up to your fears is the secret to success. Change is not easy, but it is inevitable. It is a misconception that people fear change. In fact, the fashion, golf, and electronics industries make a ton of money by rolling out the next big thing. What people do fear though is change they don't understand or can't control.

I hope the ideas and advice I presented here give you some insight and help you tap into your values, dreams, strengths, goals, and courage, so you can live a conscious and conscientious life, and find happiness in all you do!

I had a former CEO I learned a great deal from. He was tough but fair. I remember sitting with him one afternoon and it was my last day on the job. I was moving to another opportunity. He said to me, "You know what makes you successful?" I was young, clueless, and a bit cocky at the time. I answered, "My work ethic?" He replied, "That's part of it, but a lot of people have work ethic and motivation. The key to success is doing the right things, the right way, at the right time. Knowing when that is – sometimes it's timing, sometimes it's intuition, sometimes it's intelligence, and sometimes it is dumb luck. But most of all, it takes commitment and stick-to-it-ness."

I hope these tools and the EARN method help you to be in the right place at the right time. Always do your best and follow what you believe in – it takes commitment. For those of you who have conviction, I wish you success.

This is where you throw your cap!

Chapter 7 Positive Impact Points Summary

We've come to our conclusion. Let's take a moment now and recap your final steps.

- Take responsibility for your performance
- Own both your actions and mistakes and learn from them
- Take notes
- Look for ways to learn and grow
- Help others whenever you can
- Respect people's time
- Seek out coaching
- Collaborate
- Stay in the game
- Believe in yourself
- Stay true to *you*!
- Have a sense of humor and use it!

"It is not a matter of ends justifying means: but of the creation of new means and new ends."
~Joseph O'Connor

Afterword

No matter where you are on the org chart, everyone has a boss. Sometimes the lines are clear; other times not. But trust me, everyone is ultimately responsible to someone from the top of the chart to the bottom. We hope you will be responsible to yourself first.

During the editing process, we showed this to a broad spectrum of people: business owners, consultants, vendors, partners, millennials, baby boomers, Gen Xers, and so on. The people who are owners/managers asked us, "Why don't you write this for us, from our point of view?" One of our sources even said, "If I were not a good leader, I probably wouldn't want my people to read this."

I submit that if a leader is afraid to let their employees read this, they probably should rethink why they are a leader or a business owner. The trains need to run on time and people should know what to expect. Stakeholders, customers, and partners should also know what to expect, and get quality for their money or contributions. People make a business and are the most important asset a company has; how they are treated reflects how much leaders understand that.

If you have a boss that feels that way, seek opportunities.

No matter where you are on the food chain, we would like to hear from you.

You can email us at contact@earnmethodbook.com.
Visit our website at www.earnmethodbook.com and get our updates. We will be posting updates, and the experiences that you share with us, so you can continue to explore what others are doing to EARN success. You will also have the opportunity to interact with us.

Suggestions on How to Use this Book

If you are a leader, our recommendation is for intact teams to review this material together. Assign each person on the team to read a chapter in the book, have a team meeting to discuss, get feedback, and complete the assignments over the course of a month. For businesses that are interested in getting better faster, you can move at a faster rate, but having the employees and leaders review the content and work through the worksheets together can have a profound impact on your business.

First and foremost, your employees will feel valued and know their input matters. They can give input to your overall strategies, give feedback on the current structure and systems, and really understand what you need from them and why.

If you are not in a leadership role, and you want to understand more about how your business works, where you fit in, and how you can EARN success, we suggest you work through each chapter and then meet with your leader to talk about what you've learned and how you can implement this learning into your job.

If you find that your leader is not willing to work with you on this information, we suggest you familiarize yourself with the material and find an organization that wants you to be part of your success. There are many leaders out there who need someone just like you – find them and create mutual successes.

We also recommend you send us your ideas, thoughts, and successes so that we may continue to find ways to grow with you. You are the most important part of our work; because if it doesn't help you, it doesn't have value.

About the Authors

William Casale - *Bill believes that everyone should have the opportunity to do meaningful work that fulfills them, and you should always have more good days than bad. Bill's desire is to use his business experience – both success and failures – to help employees understand how important and vital they are to the success of their organizations, and to help leaders understand how to support them. Bill has successfully owned or been a partner in a wide-range of companies in many industries from owning a small cigar factory, to operating a large outsourcing business in Panama. In all of his business dealings, Bill has always believed clear communication, treating your vendors like clients, and taking responsibility for your actions leads to success.*

Sherri Sutton - *Sherri's ultimate dream in life is to spend her time dreaming of new ideas to allow employees to love both their work and their lives. Her commitment to this work is due to the many amazing mentors she's had, and the many employees she has worked with who's potential needed to be unlocked. Sherri knows that employees really are a company's greatest asset, and she knows everyone will flourish when they truly execute that reality. How employees are treated at work impacts their family, friends and the community. Sherri has worked in learning and development for nearly 30 years and worked in many industries and coached employees from entry-level to CEOs.*

References

1   The 7 Habits of Highly Effective People by Stephen Covey
2   The Thin Book of SOAR by Jacqueline M. Stavros and Gina Hinrichs
3   Conscious Capitalism by John Mackey and Raj Sisodia
4   "One Word that will change your life" by Jon Gordon, Dan Britton, Jimmy Page.
5   Crucial Conversations Tools for Talking When Stakes are High by Kerry Patterson, Joseph Grenny, Ron McMillan, Al Switzler
6   https://www.youtube.com/watch?v=m7SqJY5rIv4
7   Rising Strong, Braving the Wilderness, The Power of Vulnerability by Brené Brown